The Courageous SPONSOR

Anne-Marie Carmen Sheehan

Contact email: annie@annie-sheehan.com

Copyright © Annie Sheehan 2020

ISBN: 978 0 6488222 0 2

All rights reserved.

Without limiting the rights under copyright above, no part of this publication shall be reproduced, stored in or introduced into a retrieval system or transmitted in any form or by any means (electronic, mechanical, photocopying, recording or otherwise), without the prior permission of both the copyright owner and publisher of this book.

First published in 2020 by IngramSpark
Editing: Lorna Hendry
Cover and internal design: Liz Seymour
Cover photo: Frank Cone from Pexels

Printing by IngramSpark

 A catalogue record for this book is available from the National Library of Australia

Cataloguing-in-publication data is available from the National Library of Australia.

The Courageous SPONSOR

How to overcome challenges to get your project done

ANNIE SHEEHAN

About the author

Annie Sheehan is an internationally recognised expert in project management with over 25 years' experience in global consulting, project delivery and coaching. She also has more than 20 years' experience mentoring executive leaders in effective project sponsorship. She holds qualifications in project management, six-sigma and agile. She has achieved certifications in training, facilitation and coaching. Annie is also an experienced board director and is a graduate of the Australian Institute of Company Directors. She is a former president of the Project Management Institute's Melbourne Chapter and has served as a mentor to board directors across Australia and New Zealand.

Annie acknowledges and explores the human side of delivering projects, helping individuals and teams to break work down into manageable chunks, build their personal confidence and deliver value to customers and stakeholders.

She is the co-author of the Amazon #1 bestseller *Turning Ideas into Impact*.

When she is not globetrotting, Annie lives in Melbourne, Australia. Find out more at www.annie-sheehan.com

Contents

INTRODUCTION vii

CHAPTER 1   The Basics 1

PART A ›   **PREPARE 9**

CHAPTER 2   Sponsor personas 10
CHAPTER 3   Asking for help 25
CHAPTER 4   First aid 40
CHAPTER 5   Walk the talk 60

PART B ›   **EXPERIMENT 73**

CHAPTER 6   Team drills 74
CHAPTER 7   Debriefing 92
CHAPTER 8   Courageous feedback 103
CHAPTER 9   Roadmaps 110
CHAPTER 10   Defining success and executing your plan 125

PART C ›   **REFLECT 133**

CHAPTER 11   Communicating with stakeholders 134
CHAPTER 12   Keep the faith 151
CHAPTER 13   Taking your game to the next level 161
CHAPTER 14   The road ahead 171

FURTHER MATERIAL 175
ACKNOWLEDGEMENTS 176

Notes for the reader

The case studies in this book are taken from real sponsors and project professionals working on real projects. Most stories have been anonymised to protect the privacy of the individuals and companies involved.

In some cases, the sponsor has taken up a non-traditional role to cut through a project problem and get the project moving again. These include duties conducted by the project manager. This book has been written to empower the sponsor to be able to take up different roles as the project situation demands.

There are many levels of project sponsor and these might have a different name in your organisation. These include executive sponsor, active sponsor, delegate sponsor, product owner and business owner.

This book is aimed at helping sponsors who are assigned to lead and champion the project in partnership with a project manager. The term 'project manager' is used here to describe the point person with whom the sponsor interacts. This role might be called project lead, program manager, delivery lead or scrum master in your organisation. They have to lead and organise the team and produce the work outputs that the sponsor needs.

For the best project outcomes, the sponsor and the project manager must work in a respectful partnership.

Introduction

I've written this book to help executive leaders get to grips with what it means to be an effective project sponsor.

Over my 25-year career as a project management professional, executive coach and board director, I have worked with many experienced leaders who have been thrown into the role of project sponsor. Many don't know where to start or who to ask for help. Several sponsors have told me that although they are not project management experts, they are not fools either. They just want to be treated with respect and care.

This book will help you understand the fundamental skills and expected behaviours of an effective project sponsor, and the positive impact this can have on the team and the project outcomes.

It is filled with examples, stories and practical action steps to help you build your courageous sponsor skills.

I wish you every success on your sponsor journey.

CHAPTER 1

The Basics

Projects are a short-term endeavour that aim to bring about a change. They are difficult, requiring coordination of people, skills and resources. They take time, effort and planning. They come in many shapes and sizes and can be called programs, projects and initiatives. Larger projects and programs can be split into phases.

How most organisations structure their project work:

- An organisation has a strategy underpinned by its mission, vision and values.
- A portfolio is a collection of projects and programs that contribute to achieving the strategy. A portfolio is a way to plan and manage the projects from an organisational perspective. The projects may or may not be related.
- A program consists of several related projects and delivery of these can stretch over years.
- A project within a program or portfolio is a self-contained piece of work, with a defined start and end date.
- An initiative can be an idea or a mini-project. It is not considered part of a portfolio, but can contribute to realising the organisation's strategy.

When an organisation decides to change its business systems, launch a new product or make a change to 'the way we do things', the ramifications within the organisation are enormous. The impact can stretch over several years.

Project sponsors

The two key project roles are the project leader (referred to as the 'project manager' throughout this book) and the project sponsor (referred to as the 'sponsor'). The term 'project sponsorship' emerged from the world of project management. It means a person or group who provides resources and support for a project, program or portfolio of projects and who is accountable for their success. A project sponsor is the primary accountable leader – the face of the project and its champion.

The project manager is focused on the details and is responsible for delivering the work products (e.g. new computer software or a new retail product) for the project so that the sponsor can achieve the overall outcomes. The sponsor's focus is on the 'big picture' items: the big 'Why' (the sponsor's vision), the big 'What' (the major project deliverables) and the big 'Who' (the principal stakeholders). The sponsor and the project manager must work together to achieve the project results.

There aren't enough skilled sponsors in the world. A sponsor's positive involvement makes the biggest material difference to achieving the project outcomes, but sponsors often don't know where to start in a project.

Projects are difficult. I've seen many sponsors – some are skilled leaders with years of experience – end up bewildered, hurt and upset when things have gone wrong with their project. They ask, 'What on earth has just happened? Why did that go wrong?'

Without adequate guidance, sponsors often get stuck and need to ask for help. That's what this book is for.

Sponsor roles and accountabilities

The sponsor is the executive or senior manager accountable for achieving a project's outcomes, realising its expected benefits and accepting the risks and ongoing maintenance costs into their line of business.

In large organisations, where the project crosses multiple lines of business, the sponsor is expected to engage executives from those areas and ensure those executives accept the business outcomes, benefits, risks and maintenance costs of the project relevant to their area of accountability.

Sponsors are required to commit enough time to their projects to drive change and take full accountability for project outcomes, including financials. **Sponsorship cannot be outsourced.**

Sponsor behaviours

The sponsor is expected to champion the project and its purpose. This is demonstrated by visible advocacy of the project. They need to provide their team with direction, protection and order, like any leader on a quest. The sponsor needs to be approachable by the team and stakeholders to clear obstacles and make decisions.

While sponsorship can be a lonely job, sponsors are not expected to be infallible leaders. They need to ask for help when it is needed.

Sponsor attributes

Sponsors are accountable. They know what they are committing to and they hold themselves responsible for outcomes and benefits. They oversee projects in line with their organisation's mission, vision and values, to benefit their customers, staff and investors. Sponsors are available. They work effectively with project managers, providing timely support, information and guidance.

Sponsors are also effective leaders who are committed to the success of the project and inspire the team to achieve. They are oriented towards achieving results for their organisation. This includes identifying and owning the project benefits and ensuring the business case is clear and viable.

The most important skill a sponsor needs is decision-making, both in terms of speed and quality. Sponsors are expected to take ownership of key risks and must take responsibility when risks develop into problems.

Sponsors are expected to brief their team and stakeholders as appropriate, with timely disclosure of information. Sponsors can expect support from their leadership team, and a professional project management office if they have one.

Regarding engagement and advocacy, the sponsor's primary relationship is with the project manager. The sponsor is expected to make themselves available to the project manager to receive regular updates, make decisions and clear roadblocks. As the project's champion, the sponsor needs to meet regularly with the project team and communicate with the broader stakeholder group. This shows care and commitment.

When projects fail

According to research by the project world's peak body, the Project Management Institute (PMI), and consulting groups such as Gartner, Boston Consulting Group and KPMG, about 40% of projects fail. About US$13 trillion or 25% of the world's economy is spent on projects each year. US$5 trillion is wasted.

And the leading factor for project failure? Poor project sponsorship. Approximately 80% of organisations cite poor project sponsorship in their top six reasons for project failure. You don't want to be part of that.

So, what went wrong to cause those sponsors to lose control of their projects?

In many cases, they did not clearly understand their role. They needed more knowledge. They needed guidance about where and when to pay attention. When projects start to go wrong, sponsors lose confidence. Their work suffers and they shrink into themselves. They become paralysed, and they often spend too much time trying to figure out what is wrong.

If they end up asking for my advice, the first thing I do is listen. I take notes and reassure them that we can figure this out together. Usually, the catastrophe is not as big as they think. Often, some analysis of the problem helps them to get a handle on the project narrative.

Research-based solutions

I became so fascinated by the issues that sponsors consistently raised in my coaching sessions that I led a team on a research project into sponsor capability. Between 2011 and 2015, my team and I conducted interviews with 47 sponsors and 20 project managers.

We used the results to identify common sponsor challenges and define common traits of sponsors. From 2015 to 2019, I gathered additional data and insights, and adapted this collective research into a set of personas intended to capture those characteristics. The personas are simplified characteristics of certain bird types that represent sponsor traits. They allow us to quickly identify displayed behaviours. Chapter 2 outlines each of the personas in detail.

The insights and strategies in this book are designed to reassure inexperienced sponsors and help those stuck in the early or difficult stages of a project. Many sponsors want great results for their people, projects and business, but don't know a lot about project management or what it means to be a sponsor. If that sounds like you, this book will help and guide you.

If you're struggling or are overwhelmed by sponsoring a project on top of your day job, or if your project has fractured and you don't know why, this book will get you back on track. It will also help your executive leadership team understand the challenges you are facing, and the work that lies ahead.

I want to help sponsors avoid the pitfalls that every project holds. I've written this book with compassion for the challenges that you face as a sponsor. You might still need coaching after reading this book, but you will be clear about what you need and why. My wish for you is that you are successful in landing your projects and achieving those business benefits.

The key to success is courage. Be brave, learn some new techniques and take action.

Sponsorship productivity ladder

There is a strong link between sponsor skills and behaviour and their impact on project results. The more engaged and effective the sponsor becomes, the more productive is their overall input to a project, improving the chances of project success.

This book takes you on a journey up the sponsor productivity ladder. Each chapter is self-contained. You can use the stories, tools and techniques to help you tackle a specific problem at any point in time.

Level	Sponsor behaviour	Project impact	
Five	Transforming	Kicking goals	
Four	Learning	Developing a game plan	Tipping point: Feedback
Three	Stable	Drills (routine)	
Two	Coping	Make a move	Tipping point: Decision
One	Paralysed	Out of the game	

We start at the bottom of the ladder at Level One, Paralysed. Either you are stuck because your project is in trouble, or you've just been handed a project and you don't know where to start. You and your team are out of the game. Chapter 3 looks at what to do when you are paralysed, and shows you how to acknowledge your fear and ask for help. Chapter 4 is about first aid – looking at your situation, prioritising and making the decision to take action, enabling you to move up to Level Two, Coping.

At Level Two, you and your team have made a decision and are starting to act. Chapter 5 discusses how to model the right behaviours for your team. You will work with your team to establish routines that will improve performance and help you achieve great results. Every good team turns up for team drills to exercise these routines, and this is the focus of Chapter 6.

How are you and your team performing? Chapter 7 is all about debriefing and learning from your experiences. You will learn to spot patterns and avoid repeating mistakes. Chapter 8 discusses how to give and receive courageous feedback. These routines and habits will get you to Level Three, Stable.

Once you and your team are stable and working with confidence, you will be able to do some clear forward planning and progress to Level Four, Learning. Chapter 9 takes you through the process of creating and updating your project roadmap to track your successes and challenges and keep you focused on the goal. Chapter 10 takes this further by helping you define what success means for you and your team. Chapter 11 is about effective communication with your stakeholders and walks you through useful tools like visual management boards.

At this point of your project, you must keep the faith. Chapter 12 shows you techniques to help you recover from setbacks, which happen on even the best-managed projects. Chapter 13 shows you how to take your game to the next level using a continuous improvement mindset and practices. This takes you to the top of the ladder to Level Five, Transforming, where you and your team will be kicking goals.

PART A

PREPARE

This first section is designed to help you get mentally and practically prepared to be a courageous sponsor. It starts with a self-reflection exercise to understand the desirable behaviours of an effective sponsor. It guides you through an assessment process to determine what help you need and how to ask for it if your project is out of control, and provides advice on asking for help and taking action. The goal is to help you establish the initial why, who, what and how of working on your project so you can move up the productivity ladder with confidence.

CHAPTER 2

Sponsor personas

During my research on project sponsorship, I identified several types of sponsors that exhibited similar characteristics and traits and grouped them into six sponsor personas or archetypes. Different birds were chosen to represent the six personas, as they are readily identifiable and easy to remember.

These personas will help you understand desirable and undesirable behaviours and the impact of those behaviours on your project team. This understanding helps you develop a level of self-awareness so you can recognise and modify your behaviour to be more constructive in championing your projects.

At one end of the sponsor persona scale is the Peacock. This is the sponsor who cannot be counselled. This book is not for them and they would never pick it up. In fact, if you are a Peacock and you just picked up this book, you graduated to the next level on the spot. Congratulations! Peacocks shouldn't be sponsors, although, far too often, they are.

At the other end of the scale is the Owl. This is the sponsor who has years of experience and wisdom and has coached other sponsors.

If you are an Owl, you might like to give this book to your mentees.

This book focuses on the four sponsor types in the middle, the aggressive Magpie, the avoidant Ostrich, the curious Duck and the effective Eagle. It will help you become an effective Eagle.

Peacock

Think of the peacock, strutting around, displaying his tail, which – although beautiful – is functionally useless. A Peacock sponsor's signature behaviour is self-centred narcissism.

For Peacocks, it's all about them, all the time. They have no people skills, are know-it-alls, are unwilling to learn new skills, have poor leadership skills and often won't make time for projects. They usually last less than two years in an organisation because their behaviour towards their team and their stakeholders is so toxic the organisation has no choice but to move them on.

PENNY'S STORY ▸ PEACOCK BEHAVIOUR

Penny was appointed to a new executive leadership team. She was new to the organisation and new to project sponsorship. She did not like to admit she didn't know something and regularly interrupted, dismissed and minimised her colleagues and her project team. She made saints out of all her direct reports, who could do no wrong in her eyes. Her project manager spent months in a pointless tug of war with her, trying to work towards a project outcome. Penny eventually got a direct report who knew something about project management and Penny became the sponsor in name only. She abandoned the project and

stopped going to project meetings. She was eventually fired from the company and her project manager quit out of frustration. The project cost approximately four times what it should have and took several months longer.
It was a horrible experience for everyone.

Magpie

Magpies swoop and attack during the nesting season. Their behaviour is fine most of the time, but when they feel threatened, they attack and can be quite vicious. A Magpie sponsor's signature behaviour is aggression.

Magpie sponsors don't look in the mirror to see if their actions or behaviour have contributed to a less than optimal outcome. They tend to blame failures on others, do not allow enough time for projects and do not consult when making decisions. They often don't understand projects and think planning and process are a waste of time.

Really bad Magpies over-delegate their project responsibilities (for example, sending a delegate to a governance forum). They can take credit for other people's work and prioritise sponsor project outcomes that support their personal agenda (by giving them fame and fortune) rather than those that benefit the organisation and its customers (by realising the strategy).

Magpies can be coached. When they understand the impact of their behaviour on the project and the team, they often take the feedback on board and adapt.

PATRICK'S STORY ▸ MAGPIE TO EAGLE

Patrick was a Magpie sponsor. His project manager and most of his stakeholders were very cautious around him. Patrick was a financial services executive and an internationally renowned expert. He was very confident and articulate. He was used to simple technology to support his products. And he was used to getting things done his way.

One of his products had to move to a new platform because the existing technology had reached 'end of life'. An outside company owned the software and they would not support the old platform after a set date. It had the potential to impact thousands of customers.

The original estimate for the project was A$10 million but Patrick declared that the budget would be A$6 million. He surrounded himself with people he knew and trusted. He ignored both the technology and the project people, because he didn't like or trust them. He sent in a subject matter expert to act on his behalf. He was budget and deadline-driven, working towards a fixed transition date.

After a few months, a trusted colleague advised him to pay more attention to the technology. Patrick invited a technology person that he trusted to join his advisory committee. This person told him, 'You've got eight months left and you are going to need specialist tech people, or you will not make the cut-over date.' Patrick didn't believe this at first, as he was used to IT people exaggerating costs and delivery timelines. But he decided to listen. He made the psychological switch from doing it all himself to accepting help. When he understood the impacts, Patrick met with the

CIO to stop eight other projects so that they could reassign all the people that worked on the specialist technology to the project.

The technologists worked hard and delivered the project on time. The new product paid for itself within a month.

Afterwards, Patrick did a post-implementation project review. 'Was it always a $10 million project and I just had it in my head that it was $6 million? I know we achieved the results. But did the experience have to be so awful?'

When Patrick got the results of the review, his comment was, 'I wish I'd known this at the beginning'. Patrick took the feedback on board and went on to be a better sponsor for his next project.

Ostrich

The archetypal image of an ostrich is it burying its head in the sand at any sign of trouble. The Ostrich sponsor's signature behaviour is avoidance. They are often harder to find than the Loch Ness monster.

Common Ostrich traits include avoidance of decision-making and absence from essential project meetings and project work. Ostriches are excellent at making excuses about why they can't attend to the project. They will say, 'I'm too busy' or 'I have other more important work'. That might be true, but the project still needs a sponsor to drive the outcomes.

MAX'S STORY ▸ OSTRICH BEHAVIOUR

Max was an Ostrich sponsor. He was absent for the whole project. Max left decision-making up to the project managers, who found this very stressful as they had no one to escalate to for executive decisions. When the project went over budget by more than 25%, it became the project manager's fault. This negatively impacted both the sponsor and the project manager's careers. People were reluctant to work with Max on future projects, as he was someone who was not there to protect the team or give them direction.

Duck

On the water, ducks look very calm. In reality, they are paddling hard under the surface. They will put their heads under water to check for food and see what is going on.

Duck sponsors are new to project sponsorship. Their defining behaviour is curiosity. Ducks are willing to learn the role and skills they need to be effective. They attend sponsor training sessions and talk to other sponsors who have done similar projects. They prepare for project meetings and forums with their project manager or advisory group. They want to do a good job and will work with the team to deliver on schedule. They consult the team and their advisory group when making decisions and are not afraid to ask for help when they need it.

DAVINA'S STORY ▸ DUCK TO OWL

Davina was an executive in a financial services organisation. She showed great curiosity and capacity to learn from the first project she was asked to sponsor. She asked for help to understand what was expected of her as a sponsor and put this into action straight away. She was coached by her experienced project manager and supported by her steering committee members. She learnt some new skills, including how to chair steering committee meetings and techniques to clear project roadblocks. She was an excellent coach to her project team too, helping them to understand the intricacies of the business area they were working in. Davina was effective as a sponsor during her first project, with the project meeting all its success criteria. She became a role model sponsor by her third project, coaching other executives.

Eagle

Eagles soar above the landscape, keeping a protective eye on things. They swoop down when they need to and then return to their aerial position. The signature behaviours of an Eagle sponsor are effectiveness and decisiveness. **This is the minimum target state for all project sponsors.**

The defining behaviour of Eagles is providing their team with direction, protection and order. They have had some sponsorship experience and get hands-on with problem-solving where necessary. They are timely decision-makers.

TIM'S STORY ▸ DUCK TO EAGLE WITH OCCASIONAL
MAGPIE BEHAVIOUR

Tim was a sponsor on a major software upgrade project that took over 18 months to complete. He had sponsored projects before, but it had been a while since the last one. He did refresher training and got heavily involved in the project planning. He also had a sponsor delegate working closely alongside him. He took his time selecting an appropriate project manager and chose someone who complemented his way of working. They took their time getting to know each other, going through a few teething problems until they settled into a good working routine.

The project had a few changes to budget and schedule along the way. While Tim wasn't happy with the budget increases and the implementation delays, and initially got very angry, he quickly understood and accepted the reasons for them. He championed his team and landed a successful project. He earned a reputation as an effective sponsor and many of his team sought him out to work with again.

Owl

Owl sponsors are wise and skilled role models. They have a reputation as excellent sponsors who have two or more years' experience. They understand how projects work and where to pay attention. They coach and mentor other sponsors and are expert decision-makers.

Some experienced Owl sponsors are highly competent and can sponsor across multiple projects and programs. They are capable as transformation program sponsors (where delivery may take years or is highly complex). They mentor other sponsors and have other sponsors accountable for projects within large programs of work.

JENNY'S STORY ▸ MAGPIE TO OWL

Jenny's first project as a sponsor was delivered and got results, but the project manager and some other key people quit because of her hardline Magpie behaviour. Jenny asked for help, got some coaching and embraced the Duck persona. She started the next project by building a strong relationship with her project manager and consulting fortnightly with a project coach. She used her project reviews to apply key lessons and gave her team direction, protection and order, like an Eagle sponsor.

Jenny's next project went well. She repeated this approach and, after two years, started coaching other sponsors. She spoke at project management forums to help sponsors and project managers. She became recognised as a role model Owl sponsor and was able to consistently start and see projects through.

Courageous sponsors

The Duck, Eagle and Owl are all courageous sponsor types. Magpies and Ostriches need help to become Eagles and, ultimately, Owls.

It is common for a sponsor to move from one persona to another, depending on the situation. Under stress, even the most gracious Owls can revert to being aggressive, like the Magpie, or withdraw into avoidance, like the Ostrich.

Courageous sponsors:

- champion their project
- make time and show up
- consistently demonstrate ownership and accountability
- ask for help
- prioritise
- are consultative decision-makers
- model appropriate behaviour
- learn new skills
- learn from success and failure
- encourage the team
- have empathy
- build relationships with their project manager and key stakeholders
- give and receive feedback, even when this is difficult
- communicate openly and appropriately
- persist in the face of obstacles.

Where do you see yourself as a sponsor now?

ACTION STEPS › SELF-ASSESSMENT

It is useful to conduct a self-assessment to develop an awareness of where you are on your sponsor journey.

1. **Identify your own skills and behaviours**
   Examine yourself and locate your skills and behaviour on the matrix. Don't ask for anybody else's opinion at this point. Be brave and honest – this is how you will improve.

   Ask yourself, 'Are there any gaps in my skills? Do I sometimes exhibit undesirable behaviours? What do I need to do to bridge those?' Reflect on the characteristics of the sponsor personas. Do you have any Magpie or Ostrich behaviours that you need to be aware of and correct?

SPONSOR SELF-ASSESSMENT WORKSHEET

	Magpie	Ostrich
Behaviour	Aggression	Avoidance
Speed of critical decision-making	Some key decisions made promptly.	Few key decisions made promptly.
Quality of critical decision-making	Sometimes consults others on decisions.	Does not consult others on decisions.
Availability	Sometimes available to project manager – less than 1 hour a week.	Unavailable to project manager.
Ownership	Major risks periodically reviewed. Reacts to risks when they become issues.	No visible ownership of risks. Does not clear project roadblocks.
Advocacy	Reactively supports and promotes the project.	Does not believe in, own or champion the project.
Ability to prioritise	Does not prioritise – everything is important.	Does not prioritise – leaves it to the team.
Approachable	Somewhat approachable.	Not at all approachable.
Appreciative	Somewhat appreciative.	Not at all appreciative.
Empathetic	Somewhat empathetic.	Not at all empathetic.

Duck	Eagle	Owl
Learning with the team	Protective, pragmatic doer	Experienced coach and role model
Most key decisions made promptly.	All key decisions made promptly.	All key decisions made promptly.
Always consults others on decisions.	Usually consults others on decisions.	Consults and informs others on decisions
Mostly available to project manager – gives regular focused time.	Fully available to project manager – gives regular focused time and is contactable for escalations.	Fully available to project manager and other sponsors – coaches, gives regular focused time and is contactable for escalations.
Major risks are overseen and managed effectively. Roadblocks cleared at the request of project manager.	Major and emerging risks anticipated and managed proactively. Roadblocks anticipated and cleared.	Major and emerging risks anticipated and managed proactively. Roadblocks anticipated and cleared.
Proactively supports and promotes the project.	Active champion of the beyond the team and immediate stakeholder group.	Active coach and champion of the beyond the team and immediate stakeholder group.
Regular prioritisation – in consultation with stakeholders.	Disciplined prioritisation method used and understood.	Disciplined prioritisation method used and understood.
Very approachable.	Usually approachable.	Very approachable.
Usually appreciative.	Very appreciative.	Very appreciative.
Usually empathetic.	Usually empathetic.	Very empathetic.

2. Understand your impact on the team

It is easy to exhibit Magpie or Ostrich behaviours. Sponsors are under so much pressure to perform and stay calm, it is understandable if they sometimes get stressed and snappy. This exercise is about recognising and correcting that negative behaviour.

It helps to understand the impact of these behaviours on the team and the lasting impact this has. These sentiments are the collective expression of many experienced project professionals.

	Magpie	Ostrich	Duck	Eagle	Owl
Dominant behaviour	Aggression	Avoidance	Learning mindset	Vigilant	Calm
Impact on the team	Stresses the team	Abandons the team	Works with the team	Protects the team	Protects and coaches the team
How the team feels	Fear and isolation	Fear and isolation	Respectful partnership	Respectful partnership	Respectful partnership
Team sentiment	I don't want to work with you again. You frighten me. I was here to help, and you stabbed me in the back.	I don't want to work with you again. You left me on my own and made it my problem.	I want to work with you again. I felt valued.	I want to work with you again. I felt safe and I could do good work	I would follow you anywhere. I felt safe, I learned a lot and I could do my best work.

3. **Identify three strengths and one development area**
   We've all got things we need to work on. It's easier to be open to criticism when there are no negative connotations attached. What are your strongest leadership or technical skills as they relate to being an effective project sponsor? What skills or competencies do you need to develop to become a better sponsor?

   Write these in the table below to encourage you to focus on amplifying your strengths and working on your development area.

Top three strengths	1.
	2.
	3.
Top development area	
Other comments	

If your development area is to improve a technical or leadership skill, find a mentor to help you. If your development area is behaviour-related, check if there are any 'deal-breakers'. For example, impatience might be undesirable but it is not a deal-breaker. Getting angry and yelling at a colleague is likely to be a deal-breaker.

Conclusion

Sponsor behaviour has a big impact on the project team's morale and performance. Courageous sponsor behaviour directly relates to better project outcomes.

Conducting the self-assessment helps you understand your skills and behaviour at this point in time. It helps to allow yourself to be vulnerable and be prepared to challenge undesirable habits. Do your best to develop your essential sponsor skills and become an effective Eagle.

It is worth repeating this exercise every six months to ensure that you continue to improve your sponsor skills to help the team to achieve your project goals.

Next steps

The next chapter talks about the key challenges that sponsors face and discusses how to ask for help to overcome challenges and make progress.

CHAPTER 3

Asking for help

Sponsors are senior leaders in charge of business units or entire businesses. They carry a lot of leadership responsibilities, including looking after staff needs, managing budgets and dealing with risk. When faced with championing a project, they often don't ask for help because they think they should know it all already.

I often see Magpie behaviour from untrained and inexperienced sponsors. Many have a look of steely overconfidence which says, 'I'm the sponsor, I'm in charge, and we are going to achieve this outcome come hell or high water!' However, they don't know what lies ahead or what problems they might encounter.

Sponsors can get into trouble if they do not ask for help in the right way or at the right time. Panic sets in and disaster results. When they do decide to ask for help, they don't know who to trust. Are they going to be swamped by overconfident heroes who are just in it for the money, rather than people who can help them solve their problems?

Business transformation projects – IT projects in particular – are complicated and prone to failure. According to PMI's *Pulse of the Profession*, over 33% of strategic initiatives fail. Many research articles cite similar failure rates of IT projects, where failure is classified as significant budget overruns (20% or more) and the inability to achieve the promised business outcomes, wasting billions of dollars.

There is a saying: 'Success has many fathers; failure is an orphan.' You can feel isolated if you think your project is not going well. It is stressful, causing sleepless nights and impacting your health. Sponsors often believe they can only dig themselves out of the hole by spending a lot of time and money, but they often don't have much of either. They feel trapped.

The benefit of asking for help is that you get reassurance that you are not alone. This is brilliant if you are a first-time sponsor or this is your first time on a new type of project. Many others have trodden the path before you, and there is plenty of practical support available.

Ostrich avoidance is not the answer. If you ignore what is going on around you, you will end up with a failed project that delivers no value to your customers or your organisation. Whoever has been funding that project will see you and your group as a poor return on their investment.

In this chapter, we are going to explore and acknowledge why leaders value their independence so fiercely. It is a human trait. We are going to look at examples where fear is at play, focusing on ego and being in the zone of terror. Finally, we will explore if help will be trustworthy when it comes. Valuing independence, acknowledging fear and asking for help make the difference between thriving and drowning.

Independence can be a problem

We all enjoy being strongly independent, and we like to think we have been this way from a very young age. It is no different as we move up the leadership ladder, and we believe more is expected of us at each rung. But, when there are significant challenges on a project, fierce independence must not be the norm. It is better to reach out for trusted expert help to enable us to make quality decisions.

As a sponsor, you have a vested interest in achieving the outcome of the project. You are the public face of the project and its champion. Walking with a level of confidence will help instil that confidence in others. If you come across as weak or uncertain, that dilutes other people's confidence in the project. If you are not actively championing the cause, you are going to lose support and limit your chances of achieving the project outcome.

Leaders fiercely value their independence, and it is vital to display self-sufficiency. So, why is it a problem in projects? Business leaders are business experts, not project experts. They run their businesses. Most are unfamiliar with delivering projects or understanding how projects work. Different leadership skills are needed when comparing ongoing business operations with sponsoring a specific project.

JOHN'S STORY ▸ MAGPIE TO OWL

> John was an experienced general manager in a large organisation. He was considered a great guy and a good leader. John was asked to sponsor a project that aimed to merge several technology systems to make them simpler and cheaper to maintain.
>
> John had never sponsored a project before. His basic strategy was to work to a deadline, look at the progress reports that people gave him and place pressure on the team to deliver.

He didn't seek help from an experienced sponsor or the available project coaches. His project manager said, 'We're working a lot of extra hours, and we're getting burnt out. Can we move the delivery date?' but John insisted on working towards the original date. John believed that if he relented on the timeframe, the project would blow out by months and cost a lot more.

The team merged the technology systems at the agreed time. Soon after, three people resigned due to burnout. During the tidy-up phase, a review evaluated John's leadership behaviour and performance. The feedback from the team and stakeholders was mostly negative. John was shocked – he thought he had done a great job.

Although John was stunned by the feedback, he summoned his courage, listened to the team and reached out for coaching. He started the next phase of the project by running a kick-off session, which received positive feedback.

He brought the key stakeholders and project team members together so they could meet each other and form bonds as a team. He explained the project purpose and its desired outcome. He invited different team members to present their areas of expertise to raise the team's overall knowledge. They did some team building activities together and had some fun.

One peer said that he had never seen a project start this well in the history of this organisation. That boosted John's confidence and helped him recover from the devastation of the initial feedback. With a lot of hard work, the second phase of the project went very well. John ended up coaching new sponsors on the lessons he had learned.

The key takeaway from this case study is that John should not try to do his sponsorship alone. It is OK to ask for help and not to rely solely on yourself.

Later in this book, we'll unpack the strategies that John used to turn his performance around.

Seeking expertise

Many business leaders don't understand what is involved in technology development. Many project solutions include a technology component, which is often the most expensive portion of the project. If the sponsor does not ask for expert technical help, the project is likely to fail before it has started. Ostrich avoidance is not the answer.

Sponsors are often impatient, exhibiting Magpie tendencies. 'I can sponsor this. Let's jump straight to the outcome. I'm going to bring in people I can trust. As for the rest, I know they're trying to put their hand up and get in my face, but I haven't got time for them. I'm going to press on. Why aren't we there yet?'

It is common to prefer your own way of doing things, in whatever discipline you are practising. This is a communication and relationship issue. If you and your project manager can agree on the problem you need to solve and co-create solutions, you don't have to give up your independence. Like the Duck sponsor, you need to be a bit brave and vulnerable, confident that asking for help isn't a sign of weakness.

Even when we think we are experts, we can still make huge mistakes. For example, the incidents of death among professional skydivers peak after they have done 100 dives. They glaze over during the safety briefings because they think they know it all. They are overconfident, but don't yet have the skills to deal with incidents in the sky. After 500 dives, the death rate decreases as they gain the necessary experience to deal with emergencies. In contrast, airline pilots know never to be blasé, because they've got 200 people on board. They are meticulous about going through their checklists every flight.

Sometimes sponsors are asked to do too many projects, and they don't know which one to do first. They get pressure from their boss: 'This project falls within your remit. You need to find a way to do them all.' Sponsors are only human. If they are overwhelmed or overscheduled, it is difficult to make progress. Sometimes sponsors must surrender their independence and say, 'I can't manage all this. Can you please help me work through this?'

Before you ask for help, be clear about what the intended business outcome is. Whether it is one project or multiple projects, what is the result? What are you trying to deliver to your organisation, your customers or your business unit? That business outcome is your project's guiding light. This clarity will make it easier for you to communicate that to others. You may wish to work with your project manager to clearly define your project purpose. This is a good opportunity to engage your project manager as an ally to drive your project.

When problems arise, step back and take a 'balcony view'. Imagine you are on a dance floor that is teeming with people. You want to see what is happening on the dance floor, but you are in the thick of it. Go up and step out onto the balcony. Check if people are moving in the right direction. Ask yourself, 'What am I risking by asking for help?' That helps you to focus your request for help on achieving your outcome, and move it away from it being about you.

The zone of terror

At the bottom of the sponsor productivity ladder, you are paralysed and stuck. If you can't move past that paralysis level, you won't be able to operate well. You may withdraw and exhibit Ostrich avoidance behaviours or Magpie defensiveness or aggression.

The zone of terror is well beyond the anxiety we feel when we attempt something new. When you are in the grip of fear, your executive function disappears and you live in your amygdala, the primal part of your brain. Fear and calm cannot coexist. Your mind has literally hijacked you to keep you safe.

ZONE OF TERROR

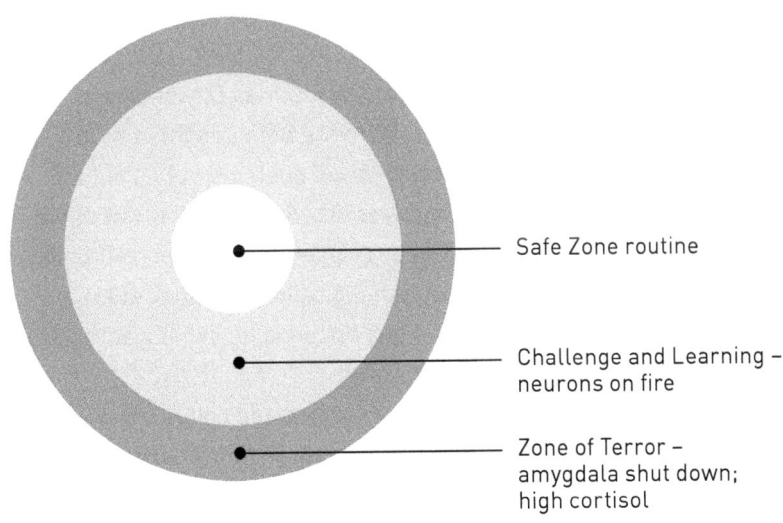

In this situation, you need to recognise your fear and acknowledge that you are in the zone of terror. To get out of it, you need to know how to ask for help without looking foolish or incompetent.

A leap of faith

Even when you are confident about what you are doing, a crisis can drop you into the zone of terror and you lose your capacity to make intelligent decisions. Fear is a tricky emotion. It is contagious, and it can come back to bite you, even when you think you have it under control. Sometimes something unexpected happens, and you get tipped over.

A STORY FROM THE ZONE OF TERROR

In 1995, my husband and I spent Christmas Day on one of Sydney's northern beaches. We were both caught in a rip. I was used to rips, so I let the waves push me out – I didn't fight them. But my husband was drowning. He was out of his depth and it wasn't good. Fear gripped me. I put myself back in danger and swam to get him. I grabbed the back of his wetsuit but he refused my help, because he didn't want me to drown. He kept pushing me away.

Fortunately, I spotted some surfers and called them over. One climbed on his friend's board, passed his board to us, and we surfed to safety. This all happened in a matter of seconds: it was a leap of faith. Staying in the sea wasn't an option; we were both going to die. The surfer passing the board gave us hope, and we all lived to surf another day.

> But fear made us both do stupid things. My husband panicked and he didn't know how to save himself. I tried to get him out of danger but, in normal circumstances, both of us would have drowned because I wasn't going to leave him.

Inviting feedback

Leaders consistently think, 'I shouldn't be afraid. I need to armour up, swallow a cup of concrete and harden up. Bulldoze my way through, show no fear, don't be weak. Just get on with it.' They feel fear, but they don't want to show it. Many leaders, particularly in large corporate organisations, think getting in touch with their emotions is for weak or creative people and inappropriate in the workplace.

Many of us are embarrassed to talk about our feelings or show any emotion. We don't want to say that we are afraid or need help. But it shows considerable strength to ask for help when you need it.

When Colin Powell became the Secretary of State during George W. Bush's administration, he had two mobile phones. He gave one of his mobile phone numbers to a handful of trusted friends who would tell him uncomfortable truths, 'to challenge me, to argue with me. This goes down to the most junior people… I had Captains coming to brief me, and I would challenge them to argue with me. I needed Captains that would say to me, "No, General, you are wrong. This is the right answer."'

This kept him grounded and honest. It was a great way of getting feedback and inviting help.

Learning to trust

If you ask for help, will that help be trustworthy? Can you take that leap of faith?

It is not meant to be a leap. In projects, people often think they need to take significant risks. However, it is rare that you need to – unless the project is a substantial innovation, like going to Mars. In those circumstances, you need to make a leap of faith because you *are* going into uncharted territories. With most projects, somebody has been there and done that before. There will be lessons from many previous projects. In reality, your innovation or newness is going to be quite small.

Having said that, your reputation and future career prospects are at risk if it doesn't go well. And, unfortunately, this industry is plagued with consultants who promise to help solve problems but are more focused on their fee. When you look for help, you need to be careful that you are not inviting a wolf into the sheep pen.

We are often nervous about meeting new people and placing our trust in them. If this is uncharted territory, do some research first. You want to know if the person who is offering help is hoodwinking you or looking after you. I remember one used car salesman who assumed that, because I was female, I knew nothing about cars. Little did he know that my dad brought me up to tinker under the bonnet of a car. I knew when mechanics and car dealers were lying to me, and I would ask them questions. Be informed, so people can't take advantage of you.

The commercial world has lots of examples of deals that have gone sour between businesses and vendor or consulting organisations. Litigation costs time, money and energy.

To avoid being taken for a ride, involve people that you trust to work through the problem to develop solution options. It can be useful to write down the problem, the goal and what you define as success. Then you can look at it objectively and choose your next step.

Next, carry out your due diligence by asking questions. Have the people you are looking into solved this type of problem before? How can the risk be shared? What do their other clients say about them? Check their references and read the testimonials – if they have an excellent track record, they will probably deliver well.

For more entrepreneurial projects, take the Disney or Sony approach and put aside some time and money for research and development (but not the entire project or business budget!), and be prepared to write it off if it fails. Take projects like Elon Musk's Space X program, which aims to build space transportation to colonise Mars. This is literally uncharted territory. Space X has had many failed rocket launches as Elon works towards his vision.

Even in the banking industry, there is room for real innovation, engaging entrepreneurial thinkers and doers. Hackathons are a great way to get new ideas in. A hackathon is a competitive event in which people work in groups on technology projects to create a functioning product by the end of the event. Your business might have this dilemma: 'We don't know how to solve this particular customer problem, but there's a prize of a laptop or a weekend in a local resort'. You can get your hackathon contestants to do the entrepreneurial thinking and doing for you.

ACTION STEPS › DETERMINE WHAT HELP IS REQUIRED

This chapter has described how a sponsor can react to projects and how seeking help from trusted advisers can help you see problems and solutions more clearly.

The following exercise is a useful introspection tool that helps you determine where you are at.

1. **Notice the symptoms**

   Are you sleeping? Do you have anxiety? Are you scared of failure? What is your body telling you? Are you short-tempered, like the aggressive Magpie? Or are you being an Ostrich, avoiding people or decision-making?

2. **Do a brain dump**

   Get a pen and some paper and ask yourself, 'What is bothering me?' Draw bubbles and mind maps and write down the words that spring to mind. This can be an amazingly cathartic process.

   Look closely at what you have drawn and ask 'Is there anything real going on here? Or am I doing too much and I need to whittle that down?' Take an objective look at everything that is occupying your head.

   Keep going until you have got your significant stresses out of your head and onto the page.

   Set a 30-minute timer for this exercise. You should be able to get most of what you want out in 5–10 minutes. If it takes the full 30 minutes, you might need additional support from a good friend or a professional.

3. **Find people you can trust**

   If you are still stuck, reach out to your network of trusted advisers. These are people that you have worked with before, whom you know, like and trust. They will have helped you out of holes before, and you will have helped them. There is a level of reciprocity and strength in those relationships, and even if years have gone by, you can still call them and ask for help.

A good project practice is to have an oversight group. This team is often called a steering committee or advisory group. Well-run groups are a community of expert peers who advise the sponsor and help them with their decision-making. They have a range of expertise (e.g. people, risk, finance, technology, legal, product and marketing) and offer a wealth of knowledge as well as professional, collegial assistance.

If your advisers cannot help, you may need to seek out someone who has the expertise and authority to help you get through it. Don't give up. If you can't make a direct connection with them, find an indirect path. If it means 27 introductions, go for it. Don't give up. Be persistent. If you are clear about your intended result and you are invested in the purpose, that will give you the determination to keep going.

When you find your trusted advisor or coach, be specific about why you need their help and what you'd like them to do. Be clear about your outcome and what you need from them. This request is a leap of faith.

4. Act on your decisions

Choose up to three things that you are going to put into action, and then do them. Activity creates options. The brain dump exercise and advice from your trusted network gives you the information you need to provide you with options. You will need to act on one of those options or you will remain paralysed. If you are stuck in the zone of terror, you may be thinking, 'How do I survive?' Identifying options and acting on them will help you reconnect with your brain's executive function.

The most common excuse I hear is, 'I can't spare the time to do this project,' or 'We don't have extra budget to sort this out.' My answer to that is, 'Then the project can't be that important.' So, you either need to reprioritise what is on your list or you need to let it go. The human emotional answer is that we always find time for the things that matter. So, if this project matters to you, sort it out. And if the project doesn't matter, I'm not forcing you to spend your time and energy on it. Let it go. But understand the consequences.

Progress check

If you are still stuck, you are at Level One on the sponsor productivity ladder. If you have managed to identify some help and started making decisions, you will have a foot on Level Two of the ladder.

Level	Sponsor behaviour	Project impact	
Five	Transforming	Kicking goals	
Four	Learning	Developing a game plan	Tipping point: Feedback
Three	Stable	Drills (routine)	
Two	Coping	Make a move	Tipping point: Decision
One	Paralysed	Out of the game	

Conclusion

Sponsors are independent, tenacious and tough. But it is easy for a project to get in a hole before you know it. Try to embrace those uncomfortable emotions. Recognise that you are not alone and that it is OK to ask for help. Find the time to take a breath and realise that there are many possible ways forward, especially when you are clear on what the problem is and what you want to achieve.

Do the due diligence on any help offered. If you need to allocate money to get a result, make sure that there is value in it. Don't get too attached to the project cost. Focus on the outcomes – the business and customer benefits.

Next steps

In the next chapter we look at prioritising and decision-making. This first aid process is about treating your paralysis to help get you unstuck and make positive progress.

CHAPTER 4

First aid

As a sponsor, how do you know where to start when you have a project that feels out of control? First, you must pause. Assess the situation, prioritise and then make a decision.

A key contributor to projects failing to deliver on their promises is a failure to prioritise. In contrast, when leaders analyse an initiative in terms of its business value and the effort to complete it, and then use that information to prioritise execution of activities, they deliver a higher amount of more valuable work.

In this chapter, we look at how to prioritise your work, gain confidence in your decision-making and equip yourself with the skills to let go of low priority work.

I'll also show you an objective tool that helps overcome optimism bias. Many sponsors are very goal-oriented and can be overly optimistic about the amount they can achieve in a short time. There's no harm in that. However, it can mean that you underestimate the many ways you can come unstuck.

Next, we'll explore the first aid process. This helps you identify and let go of low priorities, recognise you have finite time and resources, and provides you with a simple decision-making framework. Quality decision-making under pressure can be difficult. The benefit of using this approach is having a 'to do list' of items logically prioritised so you can make better decisions faster. These will not be rash decisions, because they are organised in a logical frame. I use a payoff matrix to help with the uncomfortable process of assessing, prioritising and deciding which projects and initiatives will be tackled.

Prioritising projects

Time is finite. There are only 24 hours in a day and seven days in a week. Imagine having an extensive portfolio of projects and realising that many of them were not contributing any value to your business or your customers? What's the point of doing all that work if it's not useful and relevant?

If you don't deliberately prioritise your projects, you could be delivering less valuable work or making uninformed decisions. In those situations, your team will feel compelled to make decisions on your behalf. You will lose control, ownership and accountability. You'll end up with work that the team likes, rather than the work that you want delivered to benefit your business. Without leadership, investment, decision-making and prioritisation, your stakeholders' trust in you as a sponsor will erode.

TOO MANY PROJECTS

Antonio Nieto-Rodriguez is a former chair of the PMI board. He has done plenty of consulting as a global thought leader in the project space. He says every organisation needs what he calls a hierarchy of purpose. 'Without one it's almost impossible to prioritise effectively.' He often talks about his time at French bank BNP, where they had more than 100 large projects underway simultaneously.

'Nobody had a clear view of the stages of the investments or even the anticipated benefits. They hadn't done any prioritisation on them. They just had 100 projects that their staff and teams were working on. The bank was using a project management tool, but the lack of discipline keeping the project information up to date made the tool close to pointless. The team were choosing what to work on, and it was purely capacity – not strategy, not what was the most valuable – that was determining which projects were launched and when. If people were available to work on whatever piece of work, then the project was launched. And if not, the project was stalled or killed.'

Quoted with the author's permission from 'How to prioritise your company's projects', *Harvard Business Review.*

Optimism bias

Hope is a beautiful thing, particularly when you're figuring out how you can land a project in an area you haven't worked in before. However, if you're too optimistic, you can lead people into risky situations and create waste.

According to both Gartner Group and the PMI, over 30% of projects and 90% of transformation programs underestimate the amount of work that's required to deliver them. My own two decades of project management experience shows that we are over-optimistic about how long a project is going to take and how much it's going to cost. The reverse is true for project benefits. In many organisations with low project management maturity, benefits can be overestimated by a factor of up to 400%.

Imagine a project that is estimated to cost $1 million and generate $5 million in benefits. Happy days! You can expect to gain $4 million. It's more likely to cost $1.3–10 million and give $1.25 million in benefits. You could lose between $50,000 and $8.75 million. If you knew those numbers before you started, would you still do the project?

Another example is your commute into work every day. If you are relying on the best-case scenario, you may wonder why you are sometimes late for work. If you live more than a few kilometres from your workplace, there are many factors to take into account when planning what time you want to arrive at work. Will bad weather disrupt your commute? If you're taking public transport, will that be running? If you are driving, what traffic conditions are likely? Think about those factors, rather than fixating on the best-case scenario. What is the most likely outcome and what is the worst-case scenario? Don't go to extreme lengths of death and disaster scenario planning, but try to be a bit more reflective.

Over-optimism leads to waste of time, precious resources and people's skills, and represents a feeble return on investment.

It's easy to be over-optimistic. Tali Sharot, author of *The Optimism Bias*, talks about divorce rates in Western cultures being close to 50%.

However, according to her research, close to 100% of couple who are about to get married think their chances of divorce is zero. That is optimism bias that goes against all the available evidence.

You're probably thinking, 'How did I get to be a sponsor if I'm overly optimistic?' A lot of sponsors have strong drives in terms of goal setting, optimism and hope for the future. It does work best if you inspire others. However, do some self-reflection, park your positivity and put on your critic's hat.

THE OVER-OPTIMISTIC SPONSOR

An organisation had two executive leaders in two complementary business units. They decided to do a project that involved rebranding their businesses to offer improved products and services to their collective customer bases.

One of the executives decided to be the sponsor. He was a passionate and enthusiastic Ostrich, who avoided consulting with his project team. Before any detailed planning had been done, he announced the project goal and implementation date to the stakeholders. The project didn't involve any technology systems changes, so his view was, 'How hard can it be?'

The project ended up involving dozens of people and thousands of customers and ran for over a year. Without consulting the central delivery team, the sponsor arranged for a communication to go out to customers, announcing the launch date of the new services. The project team were under extreme pressure to deliver all the work required to meet the launch date.

> The Chief Risk Officer put an abrupt stop to the project before its first implementation attempt because it was deemed too reputationally risky to go live. The project then went on hold for a month before it could continue. The team and the broader stakeholder group were relieved for the opportunity to replan.
>
> The sponsor was devastated. He sought help, engaging a company to conduct a project review and make recommendations. After a one-month delay, the team had a realistic implementation plan. Two months later, the rebrand was launched without any major issues or reputational damage.
>
> At the project post-implementation review, it surfaced that the sponsor had remained overly optimistic throughout the project and was completely disconnected from the reality of the challenges faced by the project delivery team. The team challenged him. 'When we were in the pits of despair, what were you thinking? Why weren't you listening to us?'
>
> The result was that the sponsor agreed to be more involved with the team in realistic planning for future projects and allowed his optimism to be challenged.

As sponsors, we often feel we must be confident and optimistic when speaking to our team. You shouldn't necessarily express doubt, but you should invite them to challenge your assumptions. Tell them you want hear their views.

Ensure that you are not asking your team members to act like superheroes, delivering a project in near-impossible circumstances, like the participants in the Ironmen and Ironwomen challenges. You might behave like an Ironman or Ironwoman, but don't expect all your team members to set their bar that high. It is OK to have high expectations of yourself, but the trick is not to assume that of others. There may be one or two members who are extremely high achievers. Be reasonable; protect and coach the team like the Eagle and the Owl.

Encourage yourself and show a duty of care to other people. It's not just about you.

Project triage

Project triage is about performing an impact assessment using a structured approach. Much like working with a patient who has had an accident, you must keep the stakeholders calm and involved throughout the process. Ensure that you are taking a collaborative approach, agreeing on the problem together. Make sure that they are also describing the problem or opportunity, rather than you imposing your ideas on them. The stakeholder must articulate the impact on the business and the customer, and you must collectively decide what relative importance each opportunity has.

This calm, dispassionate and logical approach doesn't mean you don't care. It takes the heat of emotion out from any crises or dramas. Clear heads lead to better decision-making, while also speeding up the recovery from any setbacks. The principal aim is to focus on less to achieve more.

Payoff matrix tool

This payoff matrix tool supports your project triage process.

The payoff matrix tool can be applied in the following scenarios:
- at the strategic planning level, where the initiatives are projects and programs, grouped into a portfolio
- at the project level, where the initiatives are project deliverables

- at the project deliverable level, where the initiatives are features.

The payoff matrix is a 2x2 grid. The x-axis shows the effort to complete – simple, average and complex. The y-axis shows business value – low, medium and high. Don't overthink it: the scales are relative to your business.

COURAGEOUS SPONSOR PAYOFF MATRIX

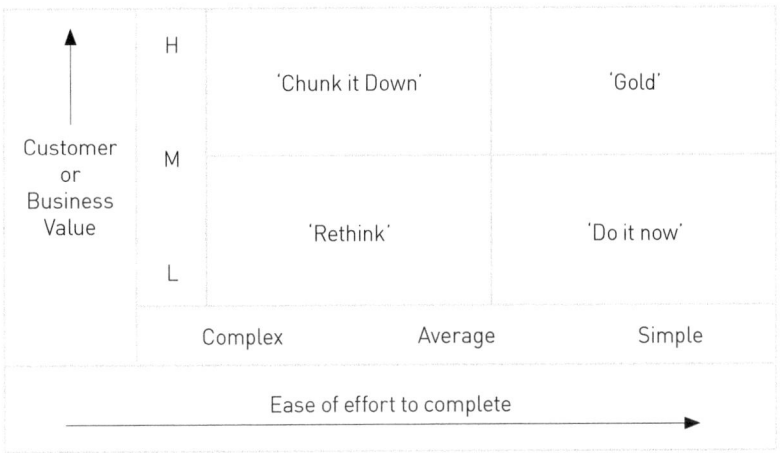

This payoff matrix is based on the Kaizen matrix. The original was designed around manufacturing processes, and the original bottom left-hand quadrant talks about waste. But not all projects are wasted. Some projects are difficult and do not necessarily have a high business value. For example, a lot of regulatory and compliance projects take a long time to do, but are necessary for staying in business. Most lawyers who end up as sponsors care about regulatory compliance, while most business-facing sponsors are more interested in sales or customers. I designated this quadrant 'Rethink': rethink your proposed initiative and either break it down into smaller parts so it can be moved to the 'Gold' or 'Do it now' quadrants, or discard it entirely.

The main barrier to using this prioritisation tool is people's emotions. Even if you've got a full matrix with a lot of initiatives, if people have an emotional attachment to one, they'll want to sneak it in. They'll want to add in the stuff that that is close to their hearts. The best way to address that is in a supportive but challenging space. Ask yourself and your colleagues, 'How will that help our customers or our organisation?'

RUTHLESS PRIORITISATION

A sponsor wanted to finish a client onboarding project. This was the fourth attempt in seven years to complete a highly complex piece of work. It involved onboarding international corporations to do business with them.

Many stakeholders had to be engaged and believe in the value of the project. There were a lot of technology systems to fix and integrate as well as new processes to be developed.

The sponsor worked with the project manager on a prioritisation session. They split the work into 'existing things to fix' and 'new things to do'. Initiatives were further categorised by 'people', 'systems' and 'process'. I facilitated their workshop with the stakeholder group and used the payoff matrix to estimate the value and effort for each initiative. The group was able to quickly prioritise, discuss and challenge the initiatives. At the end of the two-day workshop, they had a high-level prioritised plan. Fifteen months later, they delivered the previously 'impossible' project.

Initiative cards

When you're doing your impact assessment sessions, use index cards to write down a descriptive sentence for each of your projects and business change ideas. The description could relate to a significant project or a small and specific concept.

You then have a stack of projects and business change ideas which we'll collectively call initiatives. The next step is to rank each initiative in terms of business value – high, medium or low. It helps to predefine business value in terms of either the financial impact (e.g. dollar revenue) or the customer impact, whether they're happy, neutral or unhappy.

Business Value (BV) Descriptor	Low	Medium	High
Financial Impact	$	$ $	$ $ $
Customer Satisfaction	☹	😐	😊

Separate the cards in piles according to business value.

Next, rank each initiative in terms of ease of effort to complete (complex/average/simple) and determine your applicable guidelines. In technology and finance spaces, the recommended axis value of 'simple' is less than three months, 'average' is four to nine months, and 'complex' is more than nine months.

INITIATIVE CARD: TEMPLATE

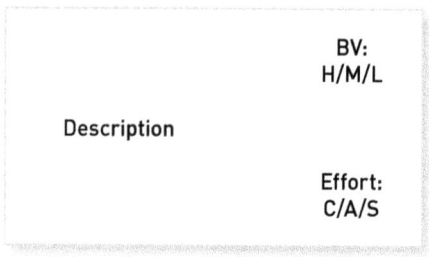

INITIATIVE CARD: EXAMPLE

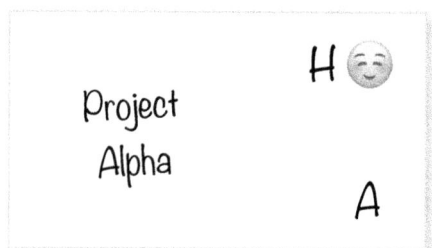

Place each initiative in a quadrant on the payoff matrix as shown below.

POPULATED PAYOFF MATRIX

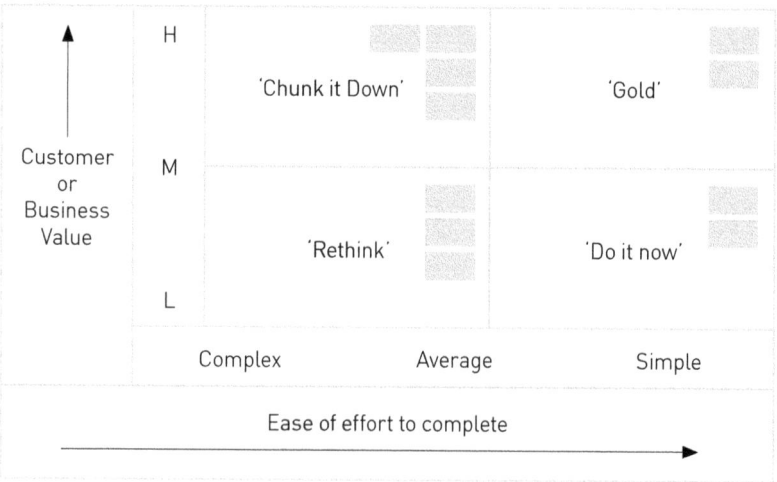

Select your first initiatives

You can now decide what initiatives you want to prioritise. If your team is new or struggling, I recommend that you first tackle an item from the 'Do it now' quadrant. It is achievable and will not attract too much attention or place unnecessary performance pressure on the team. Once the team has built a level of confidence and consistency, items in the 'Gold' column become a priority.

Look at the quadrants and make sure that you have placed the initiatives in the right places. You've identified a challenge, but could it be more significant than you think?

Look at the large but essential pieces of work. Can you break them down into smaller chunks? If you can't, be brave. Discard them and make a note of your decisions so that you don't have people sneaking things back in.

This is a subjective tool to be used for decision-making – in some cases, it will not be a definitive priority list. You will need to distinguish which initiatives are still required – for example, regulatory and compliance projects – versus non-value initiatives which should be reconsidered or removed.

I recommend that you give a numbered ranking for your initiatives. The benefits of this is explored in Chapter 6.

The joy of missing out

Embracing your joy of missing out is about making deliberate choices and letting go of low priorities. This is where courage, vulnerability and trust come in. Some people use memory boxes to store things they get attached to, in case they need them in the future. You can also have an indefinite backlog (your project's 'to do' list), but be aware of how dusty and aged it gets. Let go of those low priorities instead.

The benefit of letting go is that it gives you the freedom to focus on fewer things. You're not continually bearing the mental load of switching between the items in a long 'to do' list. You declutter your brain.

There is proof from both my personal experience and research papers that if you can let go, you will get more done. Focusing on fewer things increases your success rates in implementing initiatives, in particular, strategic projects. It also sharpens the alignment and focus of the senior management teams around strategic goals. You can say, 'That's not in scope. I hear you, but we are not doing that now, and we may never do it.' You have to take charge and say, 'We've agreed to this. We've committed to this. Let's go for it.'

Assign an owner to each initiative

Get people to vote on things they strongly care about so that you find a sponsor or an owner for each piece of work.

Sponsors and business owners can vote on the initiatives they love most by putting a heart symbol on the card. If a sponsor cares strongly about the project, they are going to be engaged and invested. They will clear the roadblocks and invest themselves in the outcome. This kind of courageous sponsor behaviour is a beautiful thing!

Your 'Gold' initiatives, including the unloved ones, all need to have sponsors. They are essential and valuable. The main reason that projects fail is inadequate sponsorship. It works best if you find a sponsor that's either going to fall on their sword or who's going to find some way to care for the initiative. If not, you are going to have to discard it or put it on pause. Be firm on this.

Finalise your prioritised list

Focus on the goal first and the initiatives in the 'Do it now' quadrant. These are the ones that are the easiest to complete. This will give the team confidence, and you can go forward.

When your leadership team is united, consistent and clear about their priorities, the operational groups will always know what items they should be working on. You're demonstrating what's essential and reinforcing those messages. If you are just as clear about what you're not doing, people start to believe that the prioritised list reflects reality. Momentum will develop through that execution mindset and culture.

One challenge to this prioritisation process is when you have a leader who wants to run the show. All the prioritisation and workshops in the world are not going to help. It doesn't matter what effort you put in, because they're going to overrule it and do their pet projects. Your best chance of addressing that is to use the payoff matrix tool, because it will give you a visual, clear, unarguable case.

PRIORITISATION ACROSS A STRATEGIC PORTFOLIO

In 2015, I helped a company with prioritising and planning their strategic portfolio. They were trying to rebuild their confidence and ability in delivering projects, as a recent major project had not gone well.

I was invited to facilitate a session with the leadership team, who were pitching 20 projects at the time. I challenged them to reduce this. 'If you do all 20, 19 are likely to fail. Can we reduce it to the four or five that are most valuable and achievable, so you can focus your efforts?'

When it came to the second round of strategic planning, Project 6 on the list ended up being first. Project 6 was small but achievable. They could finish it in three months. They used the payoff matrix to put 10 initiatives on the prioritised list, focusing on their top 4 and mothballed the rest. Project 6 delivered early and achieved a positive financial return on investment within three months. The remaining 10 projects all delivered within 18 months. It was the first time they'd been able to achieve that in over four years.

Allow for reprioritisation

The world doesn't stand still while you're doing your projects or executing your strategy. There are plenty of things that are outside of your control. Dwight Eisenhower said, 'Planning is everything, the plan can be nothing.' Eisenhower was talking about the D-Day landings on 6 June 1944. The armed forces prepared exceptionally well, but despite that, they landed in the wrong place, due to bad weather blowing them off course. Things can disrupt your plans but the preparation has still helped. New work will always come in. A new regulatory requirement or a new technology may impact your existing projects. A new executive project may appear that has to done now.

Consider having a monthly prioritisation forum for your overall portfolio of projects. If a new project emerges, you can establish entry criteria with an initiative delivery pipeline. Use the payoff matrix process to reprioritise the work already in progress. If the new project impacts your work, ensure that you have scheduled regular time to review the relative priorities of your deliverables. A good way to do this is to have a fortnightly priority review session with your project manager. Ensure that reprioritisation is considered and planful, not reactive.

This is not intended for situations like a crisis response, where you will have other frameworks, like business continuity plans, in place.

Don't over-commit or over-schedule. There will always be 'known unknowns'. Like water going through underground pipes, you want a steady stream through your pipeline and no blockages.

Commit to decisions

Use a decision register. This is essential – our memories are faulty and we all cherry-pick stuff. It also underlines the value of collective decision-making and the need to take action. Don't just say, 'That was a good meeting.' Record it and sign it over.

Many people dislike administration, minutes and agendas. However, this doesn't have to be overly complex.

The critical elements of this framework are the decision needed, some background and context. You don't need an inspirational poster. You just want a reference. Note the people who were there and summarise the main discussion points. Record the details, the numbers for and against, and whether the decision was carried. Having that information on record allows people to say, 'We chose to take this fork in the road at this time for these reasons'. It enables new stakeholders to read the history and say, 'That makes sense.'

Recording decisions in a decision register makes them more public and transparent. This makes it harder to make unethical decisions or enter into conflicts of interest. It is not only an excellent decision-making tool, it is also a useful governance tool.

DECISION REGISTER: EXAMPLE

Decision number	24
Decision required	Relative project prioritisation
Date decision required by	5 Dec 2018
Context and history	Strategic Portfolio Prioritisation 2018
	Refer Portfolio Business Case version 2.0 for full history, selection criteria and benefits
Present (names and roles)	Executive Leadership team (Alice – CEO, Brian – COO, Charlie – CIO, Deb – CFO, Fred – Head of HR)
	Emily – Head of Projects
Decision outcome	Strategic projects were prioritised in the following order:
	Aries
	Gemini
	Aquarius
	Taurus
	Remaining projects were put in the backlog. To be reviewed in quarter 1 of 2019.
	Yes votes = 6 – unanimous
Decision date	1 Dec 2018

New colleagues might want to overturn decisions. Sometimes decisions are complex and can't be made in one meeting – they need collective decision-making over weeks or months. A decision may be more complicated than initially thought. Sometimes things can go in endless loops.

If it's not going to bankrupt your business or destroy a relationship, make a decision. Even if it's the wrong one, if you can make decisions faster, you'll learn from them. Stalling is not going to teach you anything. You're just postponing it. Address it, keep calm, play the long game and be precise.

When new people engage in your project, make sure that they've got the evidence trail so they understand the reasons for your decisions. Keep your information succinct.

ACTION STEPS › ORGANISE A PRIORITISATION WORKSHOP

1. **Use the payoff matrix tool**
   Draw the payoff matrix on A2 flipchart paper or on a large whiteboard.

2. **Prepare your initiative cards**
   These can be prepared before or during the workshop. Rank them by business value and effort to complete.

3. **Select your initiatives**
   Place the initiative cards on the payoff matrix. Discuss and challenge the value of each initiative to ensure they are in the correct quadrants. Focus on highest value work – the 'Gold' and 'Do it now' initiatives. Chunk down larger valuable pieces of work and let go of low priorities.

4. **Assign sponsors and owners to initiatives**

5. **Record and commit to decisions**
   Use the decision register to record your decisions. Publish your prioritised list and share it with your stakeholder group.

6. **Allow for reprioritisation**
   Schedule a set time each month or fortnight to ensure that you are still working on the right initiatives.

Progress check

When you have made your decisions, you will be at Level Two on the sponsor productivity ladder.

Level	Sponsor behaviour	Project impact	
Five	Transforming	Kicking goals	
Four	Learning	Developing a game plan	Tipping point: Feedback
Three	Stable	Drills (routine)	
Two	Coping	Make a move	Tipping point: Decision
One	Paralysed	Out of the game	

Conclusion

When a project is out of control, it can feel impossible to know where to start. In this chapter, I've given you the tools to employ a triage process. This will improve the speed and quality of your prioritisation and decision-making. It will allow you to focus on fewer things to get more done.

Emotions and ego are the most significant barriers to getting things done. You need to be courageous and vulnerable, and invite others to challenge you. Let go of perfectionism.

Use the payoff matrix tool to prioritise. You should use a decision register to explain your reasoning. Publish your priorities and decisions quickly, so your colleagues and stakeholders understand what you are doing and why it is important.

Next steps

In the next chapter, we will talk about modelling the right behaviour. This is all about setting up the team and the environment to encourage the proper practices and enable the best possible delivery of your prioritised projects.

CHAPTER 5

Walk the talk

You now understand what behaviours it takes to be a courageous sponsor and you've also got a prioritised list of work. You're trying to inspire, encourage and marshal your people to pursue your goal. Think about the Ostrich sponsor who says 'Follow me!' and then disappears. I'm challenging and encouraging you to be the role model for behaviours that you want in your team. After all, they are the ones who will help you achieve your outcomes.

Courageous sponsors provide the team with protection, direction and order. The Owl sponsor is the ideal role model to emulate, protecting the group from unwarranted interference.

Role modelling behaviour is not about being 'good' or 'constructive', it's about having and using a rigorous assessment process for strengths and weaknesses that apply to you and your team. You need to embrace courage and vulnerability and be willing to address any undesirable behaviours.

Kill your Magpie

If you want a positive and productive team, the right conduct starts with you. Kill that aggressive Magpie and that avoidant Ostrich. If you don't, you're at risk of brewing cynicism or fear among your colleagues. The doubters in your project team might think, 'You don't believe in this, so why should we?' Without demonstrable leadership commitment, team members may work to rule, be motivated just by their pay cheque, and do only what they feel like.

The 1973 Stanford Prison Experiment talks about the value of role modelling. In this controversial case study, a clinical psychologist undertook a two-week planned simulation into the psychological effects of prison life. Twenty-four male university students were divided into groups of guards and prisoners. A prison environment was set up in the basement of Stanford University, and psychologists observed student behaviour.

The experiment ended after six days because the 'guards' became sadistic, and the 'prisoners' became stressed and depressed. Participants were all peers, equal in standing and they could leave at any time. So, why did the prisoners feel like they were trapped? And why did the guards suddenly become sadistic? The overriding conclusion was that people readily conform to the social roles they believe they need to play, especially if the figures are strongly stereotyped.

A more encouraging example of the impact of positive role modelling relates to how great surgeons in teaching hospitals do reflective exercises with interns. They are continually looking at the standards that they want for patient care and clinical expertise. They are also evaluating the interns to assess that their surgical skills are developing. Evidence shows that these high-achieving surgeon teachers produce role model interns. The same causal relationship can be observed with parenting and impacts on children, sports coaches and influences on players, teachers and effects on students. We become what we see.

There are two principles covered in this chapter: defining agreements for your teams working together and understanding your strengths. These foundational principles will help to develop self-awareness and act in accordance with desirable sponsor behaviours.

Develop a team agreement

Your team needs to create and agree on the behavioural guidelines. This shouldn't be left to chance. When the team members decide what their standards are, they typically adhere to them. Frequently, they will set a higher standard for themselves than an outside agency would impose. You don't get passive-aggressive compliance; instead, you have a more purposeful standard. It's also imperative to have clear boundaries to help people understand what is and isn't acceptable.

> **TEAM AGREEMENT WITH REWARDS AND CONSEQUENCES ACTED ON**
>
> An extensive tax compliance program ran for 15 months with a team of over 60 people. One of the sponsor's critical success factors was that the team got along and would be willing to work together again. The team interpreted that as behaving in a supportive manner to each other and never criticising or undermining each other, especially in front of people outside of the immediate team.
>
> The agreement was that you could make a mistake, but there was a maximum of two warnings before you were off the project. One business analyst repeatedly undermined her colleagues. She received two notices and was then fired. At first, the team was shaken up, but then they realised that the

standards were being upheld. Cooperation and productivity improved. It wasn't a one-off –the team removed a further five people over the life of the project. The project team were very proud of the follow-through with the firings because they felt like this meant business. They were on that team on their merit to do good work with the right behaviours.

It wasn't just the fright factor, the follow-through and the consequences. There were also weekly 15-minute team meetings that applauded achievements and thanked people for their efforts. At the end of the project, 100% of the team were satisfied, with 94% saying they were highly satisfied. Typical satisfaction on a comparable project is 60–70%. Team members talked about the project more than 10 years later and formed lifelong friendships.

Participants in high-performance team sessions often ask, 'Don't we know all that already?' Of course, but it's useful to have a reminder. Jeffrey Pfeffer and Robert Sutton have written a great book on this, *The Knowing-Doing Gap*. If we all did what we knew, we'd all be wealthy and fit. However, are these standards impossible to uphold? Can we maintain the criteria defined in these agreements? We're not asking for perfectionism; we're asking for good and bad behaviour and giving specific examples of what is acceptable and what is unacceptable.

This company described in the case study also ran protocols training for their whole workforce. For example, it wasn't your fault if you received a rude joke by email. Bad behaviour was if you forwarded that joke on to someone else or told that joke in the workplace. Then there was the consequence of disciplinary action. Good behaviour was deleting the email and not retelling the joke in the office.

Publish the agreements, keep them simple and have them on display. Get regular feedback from the team to make sure the deals are working for them and that they are honouring them.

Prepare a team agreement

Ask one of your team to organise a team exercise to define standards, rewards and consequences. Here's a template to create your own working together agreement that you can publish.

WORKING TOGETHER AGREEMENT: EXAMPLE

Who we are	Project trophy team: Alice, Brendan, Charlie, Dennis
What we stand for	Respect for each other's skills and time Empathy – consider the person as well as the task Reliable – do what we say we are going to do when we are going to do it
What we will not stand for	Bullying and harassment Not communicating if something is going to be late
How we reward our team	Say thank you When we've achieved a significant milestone, have a celebration
How we deal with breaches	Conversation with the offender Give a correction opportunity If no improvement, escalate and remove the offender from team

The agreement shouldn't be just a poster on the wall. The most important thing is to follow through. As the sponsor, you set the tone. If an agreement is breached, you need to call each other out, for example, by saying, 'Please, could you say that again in a more respectful manner?' This is not about shaming, but firmly and politely requesting that the agreement be honoured. Remember to also recognise and thank positive behaviour. Great sponsors say thank you – and most of the time, that's all that people want. This won't take long. I have seen positive results in groups in a matter of days.

You might not have a critical mass of people genuinely buying into the standards. You may get passive-aggressive compliance or downright cynicism. However, even with the most stubborn and cynical teams, you are likely to see results within two months.

If role modelling and coaching fail, a radical option is to fire and hire for behaviour. If you have a more senior leader who's demonstrating the antithesis of the conduct you want, find a way to talk to them about their behaviour. If it is making your life miserable, you may need to think about whether you can cope with working with them.

Getting useful feedback

For role modelling to be effective, you first need to set the tone for the team and then take action on yourself.

Stanford professor Bob Sutton talks about 'power poisoning', which shows that the further you move up the corporate hierarchy, the less likely you are to get critical feedback. If you have been a leader for a long time, you might not be getting any. If you do get feedback, no matter how sensitively put, it is very tempting to self-censor or dismiss any unpleasant labels that you don't like.

Challenge yourself to adopt the best behaviours to be the most effective in your role. Be brave and vulnerable and examine the feedback, even if you don't like it. If it's a one-off, you can probably afford to ignore it, or you can ask more questions and dig a bit deeper. However, if a pattern emerges, it's worth addressing. You can pre-empt that by asking your reviewers to give you respectful and thoughtful feedback. Defuse any hesitance by letting them know them that you trust their opinions and you want to hear them, even if it is unpleasant.

FEEDBACK ON SPONSOR EFFECTIVENESS

Kim was the sponsor of three simultaneous projects. She had three different project managers. She behaved like an Eagle on one project and like a Magpie on the other two. On one project, Kim had a high trust relationship with her project manager, and this project went smoothly. They could approach each other and talked very openly. However, on the other two projects, the project manager to sponsor relationship was not as cordial.

Post-project interviews were conducted with Kim's teams across all three projects. For one project, Kim thought her key strengths were 'decisiveness' and 'approachability'. The feedback was that she was decisive, and the team deeply appreciated that. They thought she was amazing. However, they also found her scary and unapproachable. She didn't get on very well with them and didn't have a great relationship. She was surprised, but also grateful for this revelation. She promised to be more approachable by making time to talk to her project managers to let them know they could ask her anything. She was willing to put herself out there. She also continued with her strength of being decisive.

ACTION STEPS › EFFECTIVE ROLE MODELLING

1. **Identify a leadership role model**
   Identify specific behaviours you want to embody and note how they are characterised. For example, Nelson Mandela and Angela Merkel both show leadership strength, calmness and courage.

2. **Ask for feedback on your sponsor effectiveness**
   Engage a coach to collect 360° feedback on you, using the sponsor effectiveness survey. Ask them to collate the results and brief you about their findings. Note that the survey is based on the self-assessment you completed in Chapter 2. There may be some differences between how you see yourself and how others see you.

SPONSOR EFFECTIVENESS SURVEY

For each sponsor skill, tick the box that you believe applies to the sponsor being surveyed in the majority of cases.

Sponsor skill	A	B
Speed of critical decision-making	Few key decisions made promptly.	Some key decisions made promptly.
Quality of critical decision-making	Does not consult others on decisions.	Sometimes consults others on decisions.
Availability	Unavailable to project manager.	Sometimes available to project manager – less than 1 hour a week.
Ownership	No visible ownership of risks. Does not clear project roadblocks.	Major risks periodically reviewed. Reacts to risks when they become issues.
Advocacy	Does not believe in, own or champion the project.	Reactively supports and promotes the project.
Ability to prioritise	Does not prioritise – leaves it to the team.	Does not prioritise – everything is important.
Approachable	Not at all approachable.	Somewhat approachable.
Appreciative	Not at all appreciative.	Somewhat appreciative.
Empathetic	Not at all empathetic.	Somewhat empathetic.
What are your sponsor's top three strengths?	1. 2. 3.	
What is your sponsor's top development area?		
Any other comments related to their project sponsor role?		

C	D	E
Most key decisions made promptly.	All key decisions made promptly.	All key decisions made promptly.
Always consults others on decisions.	Usually consults others on decisions.	Consults and informs others on decisions
Mostly available to project manager – gives regular focused time.	Fully available to project manager – gives regular focused time and is contactable for escalations.	Fully available to project manager and other sponsors – coaches, gives regular focused time and is contactable for escalations.
Major risks are overseen and managed effectively. Roadblocks cleared at the request of project manager.	Major and emerging risks anticipated and managed proactively. Roadblocks anticipated and cleared.	Major and emerging risks anticipated and managed proactively. Roadblocks anticipated and cleared.
Proactively supports and promotes the project.	Active champion of the beyond the team and immediate stakeholder group.	Active coach and champion of the beyond the team and immediate stakeholder group.
Regular prioritisation – in consultation with stakeholders.	Disciplined prioritisation method used and understood.	Disciplined prioritisation method used and understood.
Very approachable.	Usually approachable.	Very approachable.
Usually appreciative.	Very appreciative.	Very appreciative.
Usually empathetic.	Usually empathetic.	Very empathetic.

3. **Set up your team agreements**

   Use this template to create your own team agreements.

Who we are	
What we stand for	
What we will not stand for	
How we reward our team	
How we deal with breaches	

4. **Follow through with rewards and consequences**

   Ensure that you reward the team and deal with breaches according to the team agreement. Refer to the earlier example for ideas and options.

Conclusion

We've talked about the importance of modelling decent behaviour with your team. As a courageous sponsor, you are part of the team so you need to honour and behave as per the team agreement. Magpies would say the agreement is for the team to action, but that the rules don't apply to them. Ostriches would say that the sponsor is not part of the team and not be around to model the right behaviour anyway. Both Magpies and Ostriches would say "it's up to you, not me".

Role modelling is not a psychological minefield; it is a set of procedures and processes that allow you to gain self-awareness. Owning your conduct is vital, like Owl, Eagle and Duck sponsors.

The strengths identification exercise in Chapter 2 will help you understand that other people may see you differently to how you see yourself. There are always things we don't know about ourselves. It will help if you can allow yourself to be vulnerable and be prepared to challenge undesirable behaviours. Use the sponsor effectiveness survey, identify your strengths and potential development areas. Do your best to consistently role model desired behaviours and work with your team to set standards about what is acceptable and appropriate.

Invest the time to do this, because it's worth it. Courageously challenge unacceptable conduct, take action when things go wrong, encourage the heart, and praise and encourage constructive behaviour.

Next steps

The next chapter is about the daily practical activity that I call team drills. You will turn those great ideas into reality –real deliverables. You've set up the appropriate behavioural environment, and now it's time to set up the correct delivery environment and do the right things.

PART B

EXPERIMENT

This section is about embracing the curiosity and learning mindset that are the desirable traits of the Duck sponsor. The courage needed here is to show up and have a go. Be willing to learn the role and skills needed to be effective, and eventually soar like an Eagle. Be determined and consistent. Embrace a learning mindset. The primary goal is to achieve stability to make reliable progress.

CHAPTER 6

Team drills

You've got a prioritised list, and you've agreed on how you're going to work with your team. Now you need to turn up, do some team drills and turn your ideas into reality.

A team drill is a disciplined regime with a routine activity that gives you immediate feedback. They are very effective both for getting a project under control and improving a project that is already proceeding well. You can also record your results to demonstrate your progress to your key stakeholders.

Every project should run team drills. If you have a project manager that will lead this, great! If you need to lead these, this chapter gives a practical set of actions for you to follow. This is especially useful if you are recovering a project that has gone off the rails or you are in the early stages of setting a project up for success. Once the drills are established and your project manager is engaged and leading the team, you can step back and provide the team with that Eagle sponsor protection, direction and support.

The courage of discipline

Team drills create a safe work environment and establish good habits. Habits are like muscle memory – they become second nature and inform the way you work. They give you and your team a consistent routine and rhythm, which become a foundation for the way you work. It can take as little as a week to develop a rhythm.

Team drills focus on taking action. The action builds confidence, skill and capability and offers immediate on-the-job learning. Team drills can also reduce lengthy analysis.

What is a team drill?

A team drill is a fixed time activity that involves:
- regular meetings with the sponsor and project team members
- a focus on problem-solving and taking action to build towards delivering a result.

Set up

You need:
- a clearly defined end game/outcome for the overall project
- a prioritised list of initiatives that you are working on.

The drill
- Select the highest priority problems to be solved.
- If a problem can be solved by one individual, they own it and work through it.
- If a problem requires others, the accountable person asks for help and selects their partners.

Questions
- What is the problem?
- What does success look like if this problem can be solved?

- What are our assumptions?
- What are the risks?
- How much risk are we prepared to take?
- What are some actions we could take?
- Which of the actions is the best choice now with the information that we have?

Actions
- Make a decision.
- Request help as required.
- Record the decision.
- Act on the decision and work through the problem.
- Note the outcome of the action.
- Understand lessons learned.
- Move onto the next problem.

How to get the best out of your project manager and your team

An effective Eagle sponsor's ideal scenario is to provide air cover for their team while the team gets on with the work. Sometimes, however, the Eagle needs to swoop down and get hands-on with the team. This section describes how to manage the standard situation and gives examples of how to handle exceptions.

So, what is reasonable to expect from your project manager and your team?

The project manager is the lead for the team. Their core role is planning and executing the project work with the team, plus managing stakeholder expectations. Many project managers work full-time on a single project. They are your main point of contact and give you the details of the project's progress. The project manager organises and leads the team drills, while you listen and offer help and direction as needed. When major decisions need to be made that are outside the team's level of authority, the project manager needs to outline the options to you. You must make the decision, rather than delegate it back to the team. This demonstrates ownership and accountability. You can expect your project manager to record the decisions in a decision register and look after most of the required project reporting.

There will be times when you need to be more present. Perhaps the team doesn't understand the project's purpose, or is not performing or is stuck. These situations are discussed later in this chapter. It is important to be careful not to overstep your sponsor boundaries and become an aggressive Magpie and shut your team down from performing.

TEAM DRILL ATTENDANCE FROM A MAGPIE TURNED EAGLE

One sponsor, Fred, shared this advice. When he only attended a fortnightly meeting with his project manager, he didn't understand the value of connecting with the team.

Once he started attending team drills regularly, he was in a position to quickly resolve project issues, answer questions and clear roadblocks. The impacts of Fred's attendance were far-reaching. It improved team morale, team performance, productivity and the overall quality of work.

It didn't require a major time investment from Fred. Once the project was in a good operating rhythm, Fred attended at a set time once a week to provide his Eagle sponsor support.

There are times in a project when the sponsor needs to get more involved in the project detail to get things moving. These two case studies outline a sponsor's successful intervention.

FROM ANALYSIS PARALYSIS TO ACTION AND RESULTS

Luke was an executive manager in an investment management firm. He was very experienced in stock market trading and had been a sponsor on several innovative technology projects. Luke was asked to sponsor Project Lace, which involved changing the firm's investment information providers. The change had to go smoothly so that their clients' service wasn't interrupted and the firm could remain on good terms with both the previous and new information providers. Project Lace required sensitive handling.

Luke had reams of documentation and had spent a considerable amount of time with the legal and frontline sales teams. However, there was no actual progress on the project beyond conversations. New technology needed to be developed, clients needed to be informed, staff had to be trained. Project Lace was in analysis paralysis.

A senior executive prioritised Project Lace and assigned a project expert to work with Luke. The project expert introduced Luke and his new team to team drills. The group locked themselves away in a boardroom for two days.

Luke started by confirming the goal the firm wanted to achieve. Then he went through the outstanding problems to be solved. Each team member clarified what their role was and their contribution to helping the project achieve its goal. There were business subject matter experts, a project manager and legal counsel present.

The project expert helped the team to rank and document the problems in order of importance and time criticality. This set-up time took about two hours.

The top priority problem was given focused attention. They needed a signed legal agreement with the new information provider. Conversations had been encouraging, but there was nothing in writing. There was a risk that the new provider could renege on their verbal agreements, which would result in failure to achieve the desired business outcome.

Brainstorming these questions as a team took about an hour. At the end of the hour, Luke had a breakthrough. He now had clarity on his next course of action. He went to see the new provider to broker the legal agreement. When Luke returned later that day, he informed the team that one of the critical risks had materialised in the session. Being a friendly person, he had assumed that the verbal agreements would be honoured. One of the identified risks was that, when it came to contract negotiation, the new provider would play hardball – which they did. Luke was grateful that he was prepared and knew how to handle the situation.

By the end of that week, the project had a signed legal agreement in place and started work on their technology changes. The team got into a rhythm of meeting for team drills three times a week for 30 minutes at a time. Three months later, the project achieved outstanding and painless commercial results. Everybody was delighted.

Step by step

The case study above showed the success of an iterative approach to delivering the project. Luke didn't just have a fantastic revelation, and the whole project got delivered that week. Luke and his team started producing small results, incrementally. These results built slowly to the solution, reducing the risk of dramatic action that might have meant the whole organisation had to come to Luke's rescue.

Let's break this down into a more everyday context. To pass your driving test in most Australian states, you need to have around 100 hours of supervised driving practice. You can't pass your driving test by reading a manual, watching videos and talking about it. You've got to show up regularly and build up your driving skills. A typical driving practice session lasts 30 minutes. During these sessions, both the learner and the supervisor establish good habits, find a rhythm, build skills and gain confidence. After a while, the learner reaches a point where they can make corrections to their driving themselves and the supervisor doesn't need to do so much instructing. This is precisely what a team drill does.

For some sponsors, this approach will not feel natural. On most projects, the sponsor gives instructions and the team get on with it. However, you see better results when the sponsor attends team drills, short-circuits problems and answers questions. It is practical and encouraging for the team.

The right mindset

When you are in the right frame of mind, team drills run more smoothly. In her book *Mindset*, psychologist Carol Dweck talks about the growth mindset – believing that you can learn and improve your skills over time, and that talent and capability are not inherent. With practice and persistence, you can get to advanced levels.

In terms of projects, the sponsor is the one carrying the vision. You are supposed to be the most invested in the project outcome. If you don't show up, it indicates to the team that you don't care, you're scared or you're stuck. And if you don't show up, why should anybody else?

If you don't have time to turn up for team drills, you might need to reconsider whether you are the right sponsor for this project at this time. If you have the time, but still feel reluctant, ask yourself what you have to lose by trying a new path.

TEAM DRILLS LEAD TO SUCCESS

James was the sponsor of a large, three-year technology project that involved multiple internal and external technology teams. The external teams were very keen to get on with the project, but the internal team was very resistant. They didn't want to turn up to the meetings. They didn't believe in the team drills that the external groups were suggesting.

The internal team didn't have a strong track record of leading and landing substantial change. The project was in its early discovery phase, but it was going nowhere. The two teams had reached an impasse. They needed to break through that and deliver, but the internal team weren't turning up to the workshops and meetings. Instead, they were saying, 'That's not how we do things around here.'

James said, 'We're going to try this new approach because the way we've been working isn't working. We can't keep going the way we've been going. We won't make any progress.' He communicated the regular meeting times, and he kept showing up to work with the people who attended.

The attendees met at a set time every day around a visual management board and worked from a prioritised list of problems to be solved. Each team member would select an item from the list, give a brief update on their work in progress and ask for help as needed. When an item had issues, the owner would ask for help from other team members to resolve the problem so the work could be completed. They recorded and reported on their completed work.

After about six weeks, the internal team realised progress was being made. They didn't want to be left behind, so they joined in the daily team drills. As the teams started working off the same priority list, in the same way at the same time, they began to work together as one team and delivered the overall project.

As a sponsor, you can influence the team and their activities – especially when people don't want to change. Your team needs to embrace the team drills, or at least be willing to comply. It's useful to air constructive criticism, but resistance isn't helpful. Encourage the team to get involved and give it a try. Your team needs to step up. If they don't, they will self-select out or you may need to remove them.

Sponsors tend to be very analytical but if you are willing to try this approach and risk being proved wrong, you may find you get some great benefits.

Learn by doing

Don't be overly ambitious when tackling your first initiative. Focus on building skills, delivering momentum and finishing the work. Be disciplined about setting small goals and record your results as you progress – don't say, 'I'll get to that later.'

You must link the team drill to something meaningful. This gives the team a good reason to show up. The drill needs to be immediately applicable, and you must be able to see a result.

Turn up at a set time and review your prioritised, itemised list of work. Invite the team members to select what they want to work on. Move that work item to 'in progress' and then 'completed'. It's essential to record and store your data so that you're not relying on memory or feelings. Make sure that someone in your team is responsible for logging the baseline and documenting the movement each week to show progress.

The easiest way to document progress is to photograph your visual management space (Chapter 11). This could be a whiteboard or wall that is the marshalling point for your team. It's crucial to have a set place and a set time. Everyone on the team will get to know those times and places and it becomes a habit for them to turn up.

Establish a routine

When you first start your team drills, or if you are sponsoring a large or complex project, you may need to meet two to five times a week. For stable and straightforward projects, once a week is often enough.

Getting started can be overwhelming, but you have to start somewhere. Consider where you can scale up your work, including your reports, and refine this as you go. The 'minimum viable product' is a baseline that includes what you want and what will be acceptable to your stakeholders and customers. For example, in 2019, Airbnb had over 150 million accommodation listings, from spare rooms to luxury mansions, plus activities and restaurant listings. But they started their offering in 2007 with blow-up mattresses in a spare room. What are the extras you'd eventually like? Goal setting is vital for achieving significant progress and setting a long-term strategy.

TAKING CHARGE OF THE TEAM DRILLS

I once consulted on a project that involved a software architecture team. The team members weren't meeting at a set time or in a set place. They were getting their information by email and were completely overwhelmed, trying to keep up with stakeholder demands and responding to every request as it came in.

When a new sponsor came in, he set up a half-hour meeting every Wednesday at 9 am. The team prioritised their work on a large whiteboard. The sponsor chose an initiative, and the team selected their tasks and activities. At every meeting, he asked, 'What are you working on? When will it be finished? Do you need any help?'

The sponsor emphasised that it was important that the team members attend these meetings. Not all the team members turned up, but those that did had a higher completion rate, better quality and improved speed.

Some team members self-selected out by not attending. The sponsor was okay with that – it reduced friction and arguments, and he had the budget to hire other people. Work became more productive because the team was dealing with important work instead of less-urgent tasks. Escalations went to the right people, and there was much greater transparency. The delivery improved by over 400% within six weeks.

The sponsor put together a whiteboard to record the backlog. He managed this board while the team were still overwhelmed with their old way of working. They got involved as they became more comfortable with the new system. Each week, they recorded the number of work items they had completed, the things they couldn't progress any further, and the number of work items in progress. They took weekly photographs of the board and wrote monthly reports.

Over time, they could see how much work was being completed and at what rate. The number of work items completed and the speed at which they were finished went up. The sponsor could see how many blocked items there were and how long they had been that way. That helped him prioritise tasks.

The sponsor and the team were able to offer simple insights after three weeks of team drills and deeper sophisticated insights after three months. This insight coincided with the team moving from a tiny project room with one whiteboard to a massive room with floor-to-ceiling whiteboards.

Over time, they collected so much information that they had to use digital tools to manage it, but they still used their visual management boards. This way of working ended up being a best-practice example for other projects in their organisation. It was a worthwhile investment and ended up being the most extensive program in the organisation.

Overcoming procrastination

Sponsors have a lot on their to-do list. It's easy to procrastinate and tempting to over-delegate. If you want high-performing teams, meaningful work and great results, you need to pay attention, turn up and show the group that you care.

Personal procrastination is a significant barrier. If you aren't that fond of projects, you might prefer to do other tasks instead. Get over it. Engaging and inspiring the rest of the team to take a chance on something new takes persistence. People need to be reminded and encouraged. A clear purpose inspires people to keep the faith and have a go. Have an elevator pitch so that you can speak with pride and confidence to your stakeholders about why you're doing it and how it's progressing.

Avoiding burnout

Make sure that you have a schedule and a routine to pace the work. This will help you achieve your goals and avoid burnout for your team. With this approach, the work is broken down into chunks. It's not overwhelming and you and your team you can achieve something every day.

Project delivery is often very hard-driving, but you can learn to create an even tempo. Flow is the underpinning word. It doesn't mean going at breakneck speed and forcing production. It's about fluidity, and getting into good habits so that you're organised enough to cope with whatever happens, including surprises. A healthy planning cycle includes time for planning, delivery, learning, reflection, continuous improvement and fun.

CHERNOBYL ▸ A CAUTIONARY TALE

In 1986, the Chernobyl nuclear reactor's core ruptured during a safety test. There was a known potential safety problem that could cause the core reactor to overheat. Three safety tests had been performed since 1982. On the fourth attempt, the test was delayed by 10 hours. An untrained team of operators on the next shift had to complete the test at the insistence of their managers, instead of leaving it to the following day when the skilled crew were available. During the test, the operators unintentionally caused an uncontrolled nuclear chain reaction.

The original incident report blamed the power plant operators but subsequent investigations identified many additional factors. In 1987, there was a criminal trial for five of the plant managers for inadequate oversight of the test. A 1992 incident report highlighted design flaws and insufficient safety information as contributing factors.

Getting things wrong exposed thousands of people to radiation sickness and over 30 died in the first three months. All the operators should have been trained and there should have been detailed, well-understood safety processes and procedures in place.

In a life and death situation, it is better to deliver results at a sustainable pace. It reduces burnout and project failure while improving your culture and your quality of work. There will be fewer errors if you look after people and pace the work.

ACTION STEPS › RUNNING TEAM DRILLS

1. **Create a positive mindset**
   Take a meditative approach. Take a big breath in and chill. Deep breathing releases the stress hormone cortisol. Breathing helps you to soften your intensity and gives you time to clear your head. Many top athletes practice meditation during practice sessions and competition. Focus on your big why. 'What's the vision? Why are we doing this?' This reinforces the project purpose for your team.

2. **Set a regular time**
   Ask your project manager to schedule drill meetings around your existing commitments and work with your team to synchronise diaries. Agree on a time and commit to it for six weeks. This will give your team enough time to reschedule existing commitments and establish a new routine.

3. **Show up**
   Marshal your commitment and courage. This is no place for the avoidant Ostrich. If you take the lead and demonstrate your commitment, your team will turn up and take action. This will allow you to work with your team to get the heart of any issues and problems. You can then deal with these challenges in a matter of minutes, rather than weeks and months. That's the payoff.

4. **Do it now**
   Choose an item from the 'Do it now' section on your priorities list. Choose something that is important and achievable, but not high profile. Your team will get involved because it's meaningful, and there's not too much of a spotlight on it. There is low personal risk, which helps to build confidence and show progress. Then step it up the next time.

5. **Set a timeframe**
   Ask your team to choose items on the to-do list and agree a clear timeframe for how long you will work on them. A short timeline allows you and your team to work in focused bursts, for example, two to four weeks. If one of your experiments fails, you've only spent a few weeks on it. It's a fail-fast mentality.

6. **Record your baseline**
   At the first drill meeting, ask your project manager to take a photograph of your visual management space, or document it in Word or Excel. This shows you where you started from. Do this at every meeting to keep a record of your progress.

7. **Support and learn**
   Your project manager leads this meeting and gives everyone two minutes to give an update on their progress. Every team member, including you, reports on their progress at every drill meeting. And ask them if they need help. As the sponsor, you are making it acceptable to ask for help. If they do need help, schedule a time to catch up outside the meeting. This kind of immediate response creates a safe work environment. People know it is safe to speak up and request or offer help. When people feel safe, they are more productive. This builds trust and courage.

8. **Run a mini-retrospective**
   At the end of each team drill, ask the group on the effectiveness of the meeting, using a 'fist of five'. Five fingers means the meeting was awesome, no fingers means the meetings was dreadful. The target average for these meetings is between three and four – they should be effective but not over-engineered. If the meeting average is less than

three, ask 'What's one thing we can improve?' Then try that out the next time.

9. **Document your progress**
   Every four weeks, ask your project manager to use your photographs or documentation from your drill meetings to write a summary report. The first report may take some time to create, but once you have it, your project manager can use it as a template and just add in new information. This builds a data trail for you to reuse in executive reporting and develops skills and confidence in your team.

Progress check

When you are running regular team drills, you are at Level Three on the sponsor productivity ladder.

Level	Sponsor behaviour	Project impact	
Five	Transforming	Kicking goals	
Four	Learning	Developing a game plan	Tipping point: Feedback
Three	Stable	Drills (routine)	
Two	Coping	Make a move	Tipping point: Decision
One	Paralysed	Out of the game	

Conclusion

These drills take discipline and leadership. You must show up every time, no matter how many other demands you've got on your plate. It's not negotiable. Think about your priorities. If you slack off, everyone in the team will too. Soon you'll be back at square one.

Get rid of your excuses – show up and role model taking action. Get involved with your team's initial planning to understand how their ideas are going to become a reality. Speak with confidence about your projects and team with the broader community. And, of course, do your team drills.

What's next?

In the next chapter, we will talk about debriefs and reflecting on what you've learned through your team drills. This is vital for helping you avoid the most common pitfalls of projects.

CHAPTER 7

Debriefing

In this chapter, we look at debriefing techniques that will help you identify patterns and trends in a transparent and supportive way. With toxic or terrible projects, the reviews are often buried in a vault with a slab of concrete poured over the top. These proactive methods short-circuit the desire to hide bad news. By systematically recording your data, you can build up a bigger picture and spot recurring themes. These patterns can both warn you not to repeat mistakes and alert you to healthy road signs that will deliver success.

Micro and macro views

As a sponsor, you need both micro and macro views. The insights help inform your decision-making and reduce risk, leading to better project outcomes.

Micro views are essential for evaluating how you're going month by month, identifying patterns and trends and collecting data. These are done using retrospectives. Don't leave this to the end – that's too late. The benefit of debriefing after each team drill cycle is the immediate feedback and its associated value to the sponsor and your team as the project progresses.

The macro view comes from the post-implementation review at the end of the project. It gives an overall summary, and your collection of micro views will show you where you've been making corrections along the way.

Retrospectives

Mini-retrospectives are run at the end of each team drill using a 'fist of five' (Chapter 6). To recap, five fingers means the meeting was awesome, no fingers means the meetings was dreadful. Ask 'What's one thing we can improve next time?' The sponsor leads these.

Full retrospectives are conducted in a 2–4-week team drill cycle. The project manager leads these.

This is a timed activity (target 30 minutes; maximum 60 minutes) that involves the sponsor and the project team. It is critical to have a positive mindset and focus on the future rather than dwelling on what has gone wrong in this cycle. The focus is on failing forward. It is OK to make a mistake, but what did we learn from it? What will we do next time?

Retrospectives are only for the team, not general distribution. This encourages participants to be brave and transparent, and not to overthink things or worry that they might be misinterpreted.

> **Failing forward** is setting the mindset that it is OK to make a mistake. It encourages action without overanalysing possible risk scenarios.

Learning as you go

Why isn't more time spent on adopting a fail-forward, lessons-learned mentality? In many organisations, there is a significant initial investment of time on analysis and design, even for simple, straightforward projects. Many people are anxiety-ridden perfectionists. They want to get everything exactly right and have it nailed down before they start.

For example, if you are building a house, you need an architectural drawing prepared before you start building. But do you need to select the interior paint colour and bathroom taps?

There are always some things you must get right before you begin a project, especially if there is risk involved. But for many projects, there is no need for extensive analysis. Once you have completed a foundational level of planning, rapid progress can be achieved by having a go, then quickly working out what's going wrong and adjusting. A plane flying from Melbourne to Sydney follows a flight path, but the pilot makes micro-adjustments based on weather and air traffic as they go along.

Post-implementation reviews

At the macro level, the most useful tool is the post-implementation review, which is typically conducted in a 3–12-month cycle. A post-implementation review gives a narrative summary of the project or phase and allows you to gather numerical (quantitative) and descriptive (qualitative) data on a project objectively. It is the most useful debrief tool for the next project or phase to be undertaken, as the project documentation and the team dynamics are examined in depth across the life of the project or phase.

Ask your project manager to organise an external facilitator for this exercise who will be sensitive and tactful but also constructive and factual. Involve the whole team in gathering information.

The post-implementation review summary includes facts, what went well, what didn't go well, feelings and recommendations of what to do differently the next time, plus what successes to repeat.

If there's nothing inflammatory or sensitive in the report, publish it and circulate it to the interested stakeholders, the governing bodies for the project, and your organisation. If it's a secret project or the report documents uncomfortable things, you will need to do some editing. It might not be for public consumption, but you still need to get those key points across.

Sometimes people do not feel safe providing difficult feedback, especially about the sponsor or project manager. Address this issue using Chatham House Rules – 'What's said in the room, stays in the room'. Be thoughtful about what you document, so that you are not defaming anybody.

> **Chatham House Rules** are used in some meetings to create a safe environment to encourage participants to be open and honest about sharing sensitive issues. The information can be shared, but the identity and affiliation of the participants must remain private.

Overcoming resistance

Some project teams don't like post-implementation reviews. They think they're useless because they happen at the end of the project.

They may also believe that knowledge repositories are hard to manage, and that you can't extract the lessons learned when you need them. You might be collecting and storing the data, but it takes somebody with a data analysis degree to work it out.

One way to make your post-implementation reviews more efficient is to use the cumulative information from your retrospectives. When you feed these results into your post-implementation review, it becomes your research summary. It's less time-consuming to build up the data gradually, and you're not relying on people's memories. It's like muscle memory. This needs to be part of the team drills.

Some sponsors are also not keen to do post-implementation reviews. They want to tackle the next business problem rather than look back at one they feel they have completed. This is a situation where you have to do it for the team and the organisation, and it will serve you well in the long term. These reviews give your team a sense of closure. They also provide management with an investment story for their shareholders and their customers. They often give you key lessons that you can use for your next project or business problem.

Build an investment story

The post-implementation review says, 'Here are the facts. Here is what we did. This is what went well. This is what went not so well. This is what we're going to do next time. Here are our key insights and lessons learned.' It provides you with the project narrative.

You can play that information back, rather than just dealing with the hard numbers. For example, a statement like 'The $10 million project went over budget by $2 million' tells you nothing. Was the $2 million wasted? The post-implementation review allows you to say, 'It did go over by $2 million but it gave us all these things. The payback period was six months. It benefits the customer by...'

As a sponsor, doing the post-implementation review gives you control of the narrative of the project and learnings that you can apply to your next project.

POST IMPLEMENTATION REVIEW HIGHLIGHTS THE VALUE OF FLEXIBLE WORKING

The project manager on a major project needed to hire 40 people. There was plenty of competition for skills. The project required a full-time scheduler. The most appropriate candidate was a man who needed to work flexible hours to support his son. Flexible working was not a common practice in the organisation at that time.

The project manager decided to help him, and the scheduler did an excellent job. Five other team members were then also given flexible working arrangements. They all outperformed their peers. At the post-implementation review, one of the notable items under 'What went well' was that members of the team were allowed to work flexibly. This highlighted that there was a proven pattern that supporting flexible working enabled higher productivity, which in turn paved the way to allow more staff across the organisation to work flexibly.

Collecting and using data

Generating useful data

Retrospectives should be done every two weeks. Ask the team for their insights and top tips. Look at the common phrases and filter them into groups (e.g. teamwork, communication). Dig deeper to get more specific information.

One technique is to ask 'Why?' up to five times to understand the root cause. This will help you find the core elements that you need to focus on and repeat.

5 WHYS

Sponsor:	Why aren't we making our expected progress on the project?
Project manager:	Because we are taking five days or more to get everyone together to solve issues.
Sponsor:	Why does it take five days?
Project manager:	Because we only have one weekly project meeting where everyone with the right skills gets together.
Sponsor:	Why can't we have more frequent meetings?
Project manager:	Because the meeting lasts an hour and it is difficult to arrange a suitable time for another one-hour meeting.
Sponsor question:	Why can't we have two shorter weekly meetings instead?
Project manager:	Let's try that! Please support me in making that happen.

For example, one finding might be that when people show up to team drills, communication and problem-solving improves. Rather than making a generic statement like 'We communicate well', you can say, 'We solved this communication issue because everybody turned up for 15 minutes twice a week, and issues were dealt with faster'. When you dig deeper, the information becomes detailed and prescriptive and the insights are more useful.

Identifying patterns and trends

When you systematically record your data, you can build up a bigger picture from which you can spot patterns, trends and themes. These patterns then serve as warning signs or road signs to stop you from repeating the same mistakes. There will probably be other people in your organisation or your industry who are experiencing the same issues, who will also benefit from your findings.

When things are going well, you can look at the patterns and say, 'That was deliberate'. You can then put things in place to repeat good initiatives or practices. This will save you time and money.

> **REVIEWING DATA TO DELIVER RESULTS**
>
> Company A was known for having very high project delivery maturity. At the end of every project, they did a post-implementation review. Most of their projects were no shorter than nine months, and were often over 12 months. Many of the projects that had a technology component were late and over budget.
>
> Projects were approved using a business case approach, broken down and funded in five stages from initiation to

benefits realisation. At the time, Company A had separate business and technology project managers. Stage 1 was the project feasibility initiation, and the technology project managers weren't brought in until Stage 2, strategic analysis. The main stakeholders believed that the technology people would try to impose a technology bias in Stage 1, so their opinions needed to wait until later. The business people often approved the deadlines without considering the technology solution.

Summarising the post-implementation review data, the technology team pointed out the correlation between the absence of a technology subject matter expert in Stage 1 and late, over-budget technology projects, concluding that it would be better to involve a technology person in Stage 1.

The solution was collaboration and consideration. Collaboration between business and technology people to examine project objectives meant that, in just 12 months, almost all significant technology projects started to deliver on time and on budget. This was an impressive turnaround.

ACTION STEPS › RUNNING A 30-MINUTE RETROSPECTIVE

These action steps enable you to run retrospectives if you need to. In most cases, you can ask your project manager to take the lead on this.

1. **Set up**

    You need records from your visual management board (Chapter 11), a whiteboard, post-it notes and marker pens. Choose a facilitator from your team (anyone can facilitate).

Appoint a timekeeper. Give each team member post-it notes to write their thoughts down. This allows everyone in the group to voice their views, so the introverts can get their say too.

2. **Review**
   The project manager takes 5 minutes to conduct a quick review of what was committed to at the start of the 2-4-week team drill cycle and what was achieved. This is fact-based only, not opinion, no judgement.

3. **Capture what went well**
   The facilitator allows the team 4 minutes to write down what they believe went well in the previous cycle. Stick the post-it notes up on the whiteboard. The facilitator groups the notes into common themes (e.g. communication, teamwork, managing customer changes to the scope).

4. **Capture what didn't go well**
   Repeat the process above, but do not linger on what went wrong.
   Based on the themes that have emerged, ask what the team should:
   - continue doing
   - stop doing
   - start doing.

   The team vote on their top 1–3 actions, then decide what to implement for the next cycle.

5. **Follow through**
   Implement the agreements into the next cycle.

Conclusion

This chapter provided you with techniques to capture lessons learned and gain insights into what worked well so that you can avoid making the same mistakes in the future and instead repeat healthy habits.

Next steps

In the next chapter, we explore the art of giving and receiving courageous feedback and the importance of celebrating your successes.

CHAPTER 8

Courageous feedback

Giving and receiving feedback is a skill that anyone can learn. Feedback has become a euphemism for criticism, but it doesn't have to be negative. Let's be more specific, and call it 'criticism' and 'appreciation' instead. Both are useful when given with empathy.

One Harvard Business Review writer, Ed Batista, talks about building up a feedback-rich culture. Without feedback or a benchmark, we can't objectively evaluate our competence or incompetence. The Dunning-Kruger effect is a cognitive bias in which people mistakenly assess their ability as better than it is. They have an illusion of their own superiority and dismiss evidence to the contrary. At the other extreme, they may believe that they are incompetent when they are not.

As a sponsor, whenever you notice that someone has done something that's worked for you, stop for a minute, highlight it and recognise it. They will realise what they've done well and understand that it would be good to repeat it.

When there is mutual trust, you can offer improvement feedback. To improve, we need both positive and corrective insights. Imagine you are learning to ride a horse. If you're doing something wrong, it's great to have an instructor to tell you, so that you don't injure yourself or hurt the horse. It's also good for the instructor to give you encouraging feedback on the things you are doing well, so you can keep developing your skills.

Some people choose to dismiss feedback. Be tactful – honesty without tact is hurtful. Invest in your relationships for the long term. A reputation for kindness and sensitivity lasts a lifetime.

It's not easy to give feedback. In Chapter 5, we looked at examples of sponsors being shocked and feeling hurt. That's all a part of being brave. If you can show empathy for the people you are leading, it will make a difference.

Giving individual feedback

It is vital to build up people's confidence, particularly in the early stages of a project. Start by focusing on their strengths. Give a compliment and then be quiet. Don't say, 'This is what I think you did well, and you can improve on this'. Say, 'Thank you for doing that. I appreciated this. You did this thing well.' You will see them expand and gain confidence.

Feedback during retrospectives

In retrospectives, the focus is on the work, not the person. At the end of each team drill cycle, evaluate – without blame or judgement – what went well, what didn't go well and what you could do differently for the next cycle. Don't say, 'You didn't do this well.' Say, 'That went well. That didn't go well. What are we going to do differently?'

This allows people to self-reflect and state, 'I want to repeat that. I don't want to repeat that.' Constructive feedback allows them to make small corrections along their journey.

In some cases, people will need technical skills development. Advising people that they need to improve their skills can be a sensitive topic and you want to encourage improvement rather than deflating a team member. Be empathetic and courageous – most project professionals and business stakeholders care about achieving. They care about getting a good result, and they often self-correct. Typically, you will see them asking others for help to improve their skills.

Feedback during post-implementation reviews

Sometimes people don't feel safe providing difficult feedback. Be the protective Eagle or Owl sponsor. It is your duty to model courageous behaviour and set the tone for the team. Encourage your team to assume positive intent, show respect and provide honest feedback on all aspects of the project. Be prepared to park your ego, ask questions and take the feedback on board. If you do this, the team will follow your lead and be receptive to the more challenging feedback.

At one organisation, standard practice was to ask the sponsor and project manager to leave the room while the stakeholders discussed their performance and behaviour. That happened on every project. When they returned, they were given the information in the most constructive way possible, so they could hear it without being defensive. This helps sponsors identify their blind spots.

Celebrate effort and learning

Whether the result is good or bad, celebrate your team's persistent effort towards the goal and show your appreciation. This increases self-engagement and improves loyalty.

In Stephen Covey's *7 Habits of Highly Effective People*,' Habit 7 is to 'sharpen the saw'. The story is about two lumberjacks, one on either end of the saw. If they keep sawing without taking a break and oiling the saw or giving it a rest, the saw is going to burn out. You don't want to burn people out. A core part of that is looking after your team, taking a rest and offering recognition, while also giving them some encouragement.

Elon Musk's SpaceX program has been going for over 10 years. The goal is to colonise Mars. Musk has started to publicise his failed rocket launches, filming them and showing them to the public. It shows that they're making a persistent effort towards the goal.

In 2004, I was working on a secret, sensitive program that had zero prestige. An independent audit of the project was conducted by a major consulting company. My name was mentioned in the report as an example of excellent project management. The CEO sent me a handwritten note thanking me for my work. It felt wonderful to get that appreciation.

SPONSOR APPRECIATION LASTS A LIFETIME

Paul Sundberg was the CFO at JBWere & Son and the GST project sponsor in 2000. After 15 months of herculean effort involving over 60 people full-time and positively impacting thousands of people, he threw a party. It was a bit like a wedding with dinner, speeches, thank yous and applause. He acknowledged the amount of work done and the risks taken. People felt strongly appreciated and were talking about that project for years afterwards.

ACTION STEPS › OFFERING COURAGEOUS FEEDBACK

1. **Show appreciation**
   Challenge yourself to only say pleasant things and give positive feedback for a day, a week or a month. If challenges present themselves, see if you can solve them by inviting people to explain the situation. Say, 'Can you help me to understand what's happened in this situation?' Observe the benefits to your team.

   Ask questions about patterns and trends. 'I keep seeing that we've got good teamwork. Tell me, what does that mean?' Dig a bit deeper.

   Thank people for turning up, whatever the results. 'Well done. I noticed that you keep turning up. It's been tough. Thank you.'

2. **Be supportive**
   Attend the retrospectives. Remember that 90% of your job as a sponsor is turning up. Actively contribute your views about what went well and what didn't in the last team-drill cycle. Look for patterns and trends across the retrospectives.

   Support the team by actively listening to their feedback and asking questions on what to start, stop and continue for the next cycle. Ask them what you can do as a sponsor to help them improve things for the next time. For example, do they have any project roadblocks that you can help them remove?

3. **Request a post-implementation review**
   Ask your project manager to arrange an external facilitator to run a post-implementation review for your project. Be

brave and craft those insights and lessons learned into a project narrative to share with your stakeholders and team.

4. **Schedule regular celebrations**
   At the retrospectives, celebrating can be as simple as congratulating the team for finishing the drill cycle. If you've made significant achievements, encourage your team to applaud and cheer.

   Hold a quarterly team celebration. It doesn't have to be lengthy or elaborate. Take an hour or two to have afternoon tea in your office kitchen or a local café. Acknowledge the effort towards the end goal and thank the team.

Progress check

When you are regularly offering and receiving feedback, you have reached the feedback tipping point on the sponsor productivity ladder.

Level	Sponsor behaviour	Project impact	
Five	Transforming	Kicking goals	
Four	Learning	Developing a game plan	Tipping point: Feedback
Three	Stable	Drills (routine)	
Two	Coping	Make a move	Tipping point: Decision
One	Paralysed	Out of the game	

Conclusion

In this chapter, you have been encouraged to create a culture of authentic feedback, both positive and corrective. We looked at focusing on constructive feedback and shifting your mindset and language in that direction. We also stressed the importance of celebrating effort and thanking your team.

Resist impatience and the urge to 'just get on with it'. Ensure that you schedule time for feedback, reviews and celebrations. Don't skip them. Focus equally on the lessons learned and the achievements. That way you won't be a nitpicking Magpie.

Next steps

The next chapter talks about developing your longer-term game plan with strategic roadmaps. You've done your team drills, performed post-practice debriefs and reviewed the lessons learned. Now it's time to up the ante.

CHAPTER 9

Roadmaps

You've got one or more of your significant projects under control. You've established some team drills, which will lead to good habits. You're learning from your efforts, spotting patterns and avoiding many pitfalls. This is courageous sponsor behaviour, exhibited by Ducks, Eagles and Owls.

If you want to move beyond a reactive environment to a more proactive one, you have to understand what you need to sacrifice, and you will have to put in time and effort to achieve it. What will it mean to operate at that higher level? You may need to do some soul searching. Are you willing to do the work, build that capability, make the time and create the capacity to get there? If so, you will need a plan. Wishing will get you nowhere.

This chapter takes you through the process of defining your longer-term game plan. You will develop a visual roadmap of your project work that shows your end goal, identifies the stepping stones that will help you get there, and describes the approach you will need to take.

What is a roadmap?

A roadmap is an overall plan from which further, more detailed plans can be developed. It is a visual representation of your project work, with supporting descriptions. A good roadmap can be easily explained by the owner and easily understood by the project team and stakeholders. It is just as useful for small projects as substantial ones.

Elements in a roadmap:

- Your guiding light: the project purpose.
- Macro prioritised plan and schedule linked to your purpose

CREATING AND USING ROADMAPS

One of my roles involved mentoring seven different PMI (Project Management Institute) chapter boards across Australia and New Zealand. Each chapter had its own defined purpose, linked to the overall PMI purpose. PMI's purpose was to help project professionals and organisations get better at converting strategic ideas to operational reality. Each chapter had 6-12 volunteer directors on each board. Each volunteer had a personal purpose and reason for volunteering.

Prior to 2018, each chapter had very different annual plans and needed to refocus on a set of core customer services. I facilitated each chapter's planning days. Before the planning day, PMI staff provided a standardised list of core services to their chapter directors. The directors reviewed the services and made a note of any they had to maintain, ones they wanted to improve and new initiatives they would like to implement. On the day, the new and improvement initiatives were prioritised using the payoff matrix. The top priority initiatives were then placed on the roadmap timeline.

One group of chapter directors was very enthusiastic and tried to put all the new pieces of work into the first and second quarters. The directors were then asked to consider routine tasks and see what impact they had on the schedule. The work items were subsequently spread out across all four quarters.

Then the group was asked to consider unexpected events ('surprises'). What would they do if a new mandatory piece of work came in? What if the lead volunteer on an initiative left? This helped the team further prioritise the list to understand which initiatives they would cancel or deprioritise if needed.

One new event idea was a project management day of service (PMDOS). This was a one-day event where PMI members offered their professional project services to help charities develop plans, budgets and other collateral for their projects. The effort involved in organising this event was like holding a small wedding. Venue, budget, guests and suppliers all had to be identified and worked out in detail. Was running PMDOS essential for that year, or could it wait? Some chapters chose to run PMDOS as a priority, some deferred.

This type of roadmap planning ensured each chapter delivered what was required of them and had contingency for some local flavour.

Identify your guiding light

Start with purpose and vision. A clearly defined purpose is your guiding light –this is the overall corporate vision that tells you where you're going. Enrich your project purpose by linking this to the organisational mission.

When you are developing your game plan, it is a critical part to have your end goal in mind. That is your compelling purpose. Here, we have used a lighthouse to represent this. Know what your destination is before you start your journey. Understand the compelling 'why' that will keep you going. These are your guiding lights. The path is not carved out, but there are clear stepping stones along the way.

The power of purpose

Simon Sinek is the author of *Start With Why*. His Golden Circles model starts with 'Why' in the middle, then moves to 'How' and 'What'. By 'Why' he means, 'What is your purpose, cause or belief? Why does your company exist? Why do you get out of bed every morning? Why should anyone care?'

There is a lot of human emotion and feelings tied into the 'Why'. Sinek relates this to our brains. We talked about amygdalas and executive function in Chapter 3. Your 'Why' connects your limbic brain, feelings and emotions, which is where you make gut decisions. To quote Sinek, 'Our limbic brain is powerful. Powerful enough to drive behaviour that sometimes contradicts our rational and analytical understanding of the situation.'

Understanding how your compelling purpose connects to the corporate mission is vital. Sponsors are high achievers, motivated, success-driven and stewards of organisational resources. The roadmap below shows you at the start of your journey. In this example, your roadmap is divided into five quarters (the triangles represent 90-day time markers) to reach your guiding light.

INCOMPLETE ROADMAP

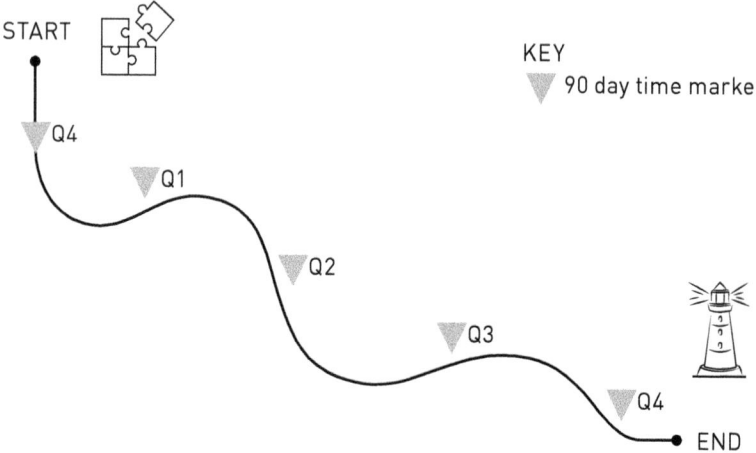

You might be thinking, 'I know where I'm going. I've got my lighthouse at the end. I know that I'm going to be getting there in roughly a year and a half. How am I going to get there?' Having that guiding light and purpose helps you keep going when you hit a roadblock, or when you get disheartened. It also gives you some guard rails to help keep you on the right track.

We explored decision-making in Chapter 4. If you are tackling a situation without having a clear 'Why' in mind, a decision is hard to make. The 'Why' helps your decision-making be faster and better.

COMPELLING PURPOSE

When Bill Gates founded Microsoft in 1975, a time when there were hardly any personal computers, he was passionate about his vision of a computer being on every desk and in every home. From our perspective today, with computers and smartphones everywhere, Gates completely overshot on his compelling purpose.

Harnessing your personal purpose

Your role as a sponsor is to strengthen everyone's individual purpose so they connect with you at a deep level. This builds trust and loyalty, which helps your team's effectiveness.

Start with tying your personal purpose to your project's purpose. Think about why you're turning up and how you, as an individual, will benefit from delivering the project. Think about the skills you will acquire, your potential achievements and your potential to help others. What are you going to get out of it?

Work with your team to understand your collective purpose. You may wish to engage a facilitator to help you with this. Questions to ask include:
- What is the team's purpose? As a sponsor, it's helpful to think about yourself and your group as a collective.
- How is the company going to benefit? You are probably working for an organisation that wants more than just a project delivered.
- What are the useful extras you can deliver to benefit the organisation? Tie these to the company purpose.

Sometimes sponsors worry that purpose is beyond their remit or is not what they care about. If this is you, you might be overthinking it. Ask yourself how every aspect of your life will benefit from delivering this project, not just your career. Your goal might be to be the breadwinner for your family while your children are young. If you seek more purpose than your work, perhaps there is a volunteer project or hobby that adds meaning to your life. It doesn't all have to be within the work context.

ACHIEVING ORGANISATIONAL KPIS FOR A MULTI-YEAR STRATEGIC PLAN

AXA took over an Australian company called National Mutual in 1999. The incoming CEO had a multi-year strategic plan that he called K5. They had a strategic vision and the key performance indicators were displayed everywhere. Everyone was clear on the vision and key performance indicators because they were in every meeting room, the staircases and the lifts. It helped to reinforce the messages.

It was going to be challenging, but everyone understood where it was heading. Every project belonged to a portfolio. Each portfolio linked to the overall company strategy. Sponsors, supported by project managers, used a business case template to write up the principal details for each project. These details included what the project was going to deliver, the benefits for customers and the organisation, and how it would help realise that strategy.

Staff knew every day that their work had meaning and was directly connected to the outcomes. One project was a sales commission system that replaced a printed letter system sent to the advisers. This was linked to a strategic goal for AXA to be consistently ranked in the top five companies for service to advisers. The new system was a big hit with advisers and became one of their most popular tools.

After five years, the executive leaders achieved their outcomes and created a new five-year strategy called AXA 6.

Define your stepping stones

You need a macro-level prioritised plan and schedule. Work with your project manager to use the payoff matrix tool from Chapter 4 to create your stepping stones. Your project manager will lead this activity.

Example stepping stones
Lighthouse – A new bank card facility

- Move existing product from one technology platform to another.
- Develop critical features.
- Develop second feature set.
- Start marketing campaign.
- Develop third feature set.
- Launch product.
- Complete business handover.

THE VALUE OF MONTHLY MACRO PLANNING

Company B decided to upgrade their technology infrastructure and the way that they carried out technology projects and capability. They hired a new CIO, Peter, to transform the technology department, improve their project delivery ability and generate a better return on investment for the organisation and its customers. They had had mixed success delivering large projects before then.

One of the things that Peter brought in was a project management discipline. His macro plan was a portfolio of projects. Every month, Company B held a steering committee forum with the group executive, who prioritised the projects. The executives gave the green light to a maximum of 50 projects on the list. They put everything else in a backlog. The focus was on the top five projects, then the next 10.

They published the priority list every month, so everybody knew what the top five projects were and where to pay attention. The rule was that a project with a higher priority could – and did – take resources (usually skilled people) from a lower-priority project. On some occasions, lower-priority projects were paused or killed off. It was very effective, delivering the highest priority projects consistently.

Many business transformation programs fail because their outcomes are too far into the future. Stepping stones and time increments make the outcomes appear less overwhelming and more achievable. It also makes it easier for the sponsor to oversee the project.

ACTION STEPS ▸ PRODUCE A DRAFT ROADMAP

Produce a draft roadmap to give you, your team and your stakeholders a snapshot of your overall plan to give them a level of confidence and certainty.

1. **Preparation**
- Engage a facilitator to set this up for you.
- Using the payoff matrix tool from Chapter 4, select and prioritise your projects, programs and business initiatives. Post-it notes are helpful. Prioritise them using the grid.
- Identify your non-project work (e.g. business operations, weekly company meetings) and how much time this takes.

2. **Process**
- Set aside time with your team. If this is the first time that you have created a roadmap, start with 2–3 hours. The minimum is 2 hours, but you might need a few days, depending on complexity.
- You will need a whiteboard or butchers' paper, markers and post-it notes.
- Draw a squiggly line to represent your road and label the start and the end. Place time markers at 90-day intervals on your 'road'.
- Place the prioritised items from your payoff matrix on your roadmap timeline. Start with your 'Gold' and 'Do it now' items. These are your stepping stones.
- Work on the most important projects first. Remember the optimism bias we discussed in Chapter 4? It is human nature to want to do everything early.
- A word of caution: don't get into detailed planning in the macro plan. Save that for the prioritisation and team drill sessions that we discussed in Chapters 4 and 6.

DRAFT ROADMAP WITH TIME MARKERS, STEPPING STONES AND GUIDING LIGHT

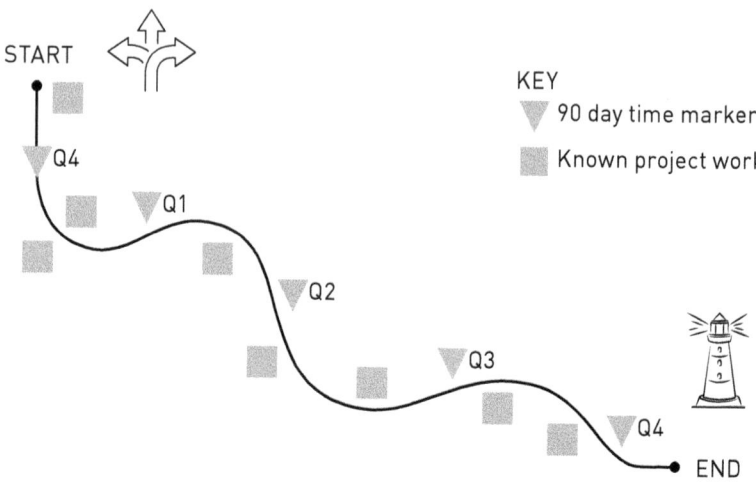

Pacing the work

Ensure the plan is not over-ambitious, that normal daily activity is factored in and you have an agreement on how to handle unexpected events. At one extreme, I have facilitated sessions with enthusiastic sponsors who overload their plans and forget to factor in time for sleep!

PACING THE WORK IN A MATURE PROJECT ENVIRONMENT

AXA's project community was considered best-in-class for project management. In 2008, they had an 87% success rate on project portfolio delivery when, at that time, most organisations were at about 40%.

They had a 68% staff engagement score from their project team, which they thought was low. By industry standards, 68% was considered high but compared to the rest of the organisation, it was short. Project professionals set high standards and expect a lot from themselves.

AXA scheduled annual planning cycles and funding stages. Every month, they ran funding and decision-making forums where projects were approved. They had communities of practice for business analysis, change management and project management. Every person's scorecard linked to the strategy. Every project related to the strategic outcome. People were doing, learning and reflecting in a planned virtuous cycle.

ACTION STEPS › NOTE ROUTINE ACTIVITY AND SURPRISES ON YOUR ROADMAP

1. **Schedule major meetings**
   This is good operating and calendar practice. Book in your significant regular get-togethers, such as governance and oversight forums, roadshows and annual planning. Use these opportunities to support your team and schedule regular times for learning.

2. **Support learning**
   Support your project manager to schedule 2 hours a fortnight for team skills development. This time will give your group noticeable skills improvement. This learning time can fit within your team drill cycle. Some sponsors also attend these sessions.

3. **Factor in absences**
   It is easy to forget about public holidays and annual leave, so check with your project manager that these are factored in.

4. **Agree on how to manage surprises**
   Work with your project manager on an approved assessment approach for dealing with material changes to your plans and schedules. These are the 'surprises' in the roadmap. You don't have to imagine every single disaster. Try and keep it realistic. Ask your team:
   - What could go wrong?
   - If it does go wrong, what do we need to do to fix it?
   - Do we need to keep some money in reserve?
   - Do we need more flexibility in our schedule?
   - What will we do if significant problems arise?

   As a sponsor, you hold the purse strings. What approvals and assurances can you give your team? Agree what decisions

your team can make without reference to the sponsor. When do they have to come to you for a decision? Document your answers and work out how you're going to adjust your plans.

5. **Schedule time in your team drills for essential activities**
   These activities could include:
   - accepting changes and adapting plans
   - team learning
   - reflection and continuous improvement.

6. **Schedule appreciation activities**
   Don't underestimate the power of taking the team out to lunch or hosting a morning tea to acknowledge their efforts. Schedule an appreciation activity, like team drinks, or take people out for mini-golf or another fun activity. Remember to say thank you. A little bit of appreciation goes a very long way.

COMPLETED ROADMAP WITH CALLOUTS FOR ROUTINE WORK AND SURPRISES

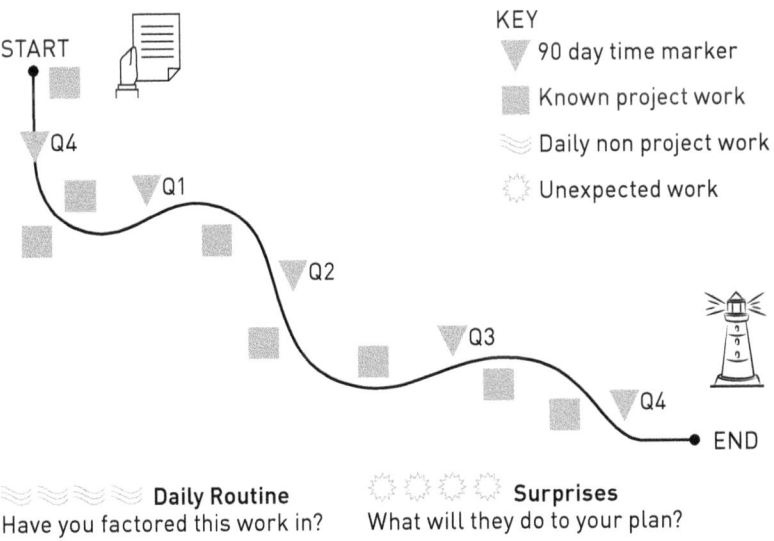

7. **Display your completed roadmap**
   This shows you, your team and your stakeholders your target and your intention. It gives them confidence that there is a clear plan.

   Your completed roadmap is your baseline. A baseline in a project is a clearly defined reference point to measure and compare your project's progress against. It allows you to assess the performance of your project over time. It shows what you have planned. As you update it with what really happened ('actuals'), you will see how accurate your planning predictions were. Updating your roadmap is covered in Chapter 12.

Conclusion

Resist executive impatience. Don't rush the process. Ignore the pressure to 'Just do it'. Planning is essential, even at the micro-level. Plenty of research identifies inadequate planning as a cause of project failure. We're looking for Goldilocks planning here: not too much, and not too little.

Projects are created to achieve corporate goals. Without that active link to strategy, the human desire to start new projects or focus on ones that have personal appeal is strong. If your stepping stones are not clearly linked to strategic corporate goals, they might lead you to the wrong destination.

Next steps

The next chapter will help you define success at the beginning of your project and measure it at the end.

CHAPTER 10

Defining success and executing your plan

You've made it to the end of the year and you've delivered 25 projects. But if you only measure your accomplishments at the end, how do you know if you've been successful? In this chapter, we discuss two models that will help you define success and measure success.

Defining success at the start of a project helps us to know what's most valuable when making decisions along the way. It gives you objective measures to look at when you're conducting your post-implementation review. Has the project really been successful? Or are you rewriting history in your favour? For example, if working to a fixed budget is important, then failure would be exceeding that budget.

Success on long-term projects

Large transformation programs tend to go for years. Even if success is well-defined at the beginning, many factors will change (e.g. economic, environmental, company restructures). There are many elements you can't control when projects last more than 12 months. It is better to define success measures for each phase, and then contain each of the stages to a maximum of 12 months.

Have clarity on what success looks like to you. Define your success criteria from this point onwards. In Chapter 3, we discussed moving from the zone of terror into rational thought processes. You acknowledged your fears, asked for help and took action. Now that your project is in a stable state, you can be clear-headed about defining your success criteria.

There are many success models and each has its merits. In this chapter, we are going to look at two models. At the strategic portfolio and program level, the balanced scorecard has been used to great effect. At the individual project level, descriptive critical success factors related to project knowledge areas (e.g. time, cost, quality, stakeholders) have been the most effective.

Balanced scorecard

The balanced scorecard is a very effective descriptive success tool. It has vision and strategy at the centre, with success defined as a balance between finance, customer, internal business processes, and learning and growth. For example, you can't have outstanding financial results at the expense of poor customer outcomes, or no learning and growth for your staff.

DEFINING SUCCESS USING A BALANCED SCORECARD

When JBWere & Son upgraded their technology infrastructure back in the late 1990s, the CIO used a balanced scorecard to define success and engage the executive leaders in agreeing to the relative priority of each of the projects in the company's portfolio. The primary success factors were focused on client satisfaction, followed by financial return on investment. These were balanced with consideration for sustainable business processes and benefits to staff.

It is rare for projects to be prioritised in this way, with this amount of senior buy-in. Everybody was clear about the relative importance of the various success factors. JBWere had a strong values focus, so service to the clients and the advisers came first. This customer-focused concept became popular about 15 years later, so JBWere were ahead of the trend.

Critical success factors

What elements must you have that define success for your project? Most projects define success as all of the agreed scope being delivered on time, under budget and to quality standards. However, many organisations would still declare a project successful if it was late or over budget, provided it achieved a useful outcome and some customer benefits. This is where critical success factors come in. What are the *most* important measures that must be met to declare your project a success?

DEFINING SUCCESS USING CRITICAL SUCCESS FACTORS

A significant compliance program was sponsored by the organisation's CFO. He defined four critical success factors. He wanted minimum disruption to the business for clients and advisers so that they barely noticed the project work going on around them. He wanted to achieve compliance by the set dates. Teamwork was essential, and he wanted to make sure that the team treated each other well and were willing to work together again. He was soft on the project costs, saying, 'Tell us how much you think it's going to cost, and we'll write the cheques'. The project manager was given six months to come up with a final budget, for which they were then held accountable.

At the project's conclusion, the project achieved all the success factors. The executive team celebrated the minimal disruption to the business and the compliance on the dates. The sponsor was pleased that it was 10% under budget, and the team formed strong bonds that lasted for many years.

ACTION STEPS › DEFINING SUCCESS FACTORS

Engage a facilitator to run a strategic planning workshop for you and your major stakeholders to help you define and prioritise your critical success factors. This is a fast-paced process, designed to give a high-level view of success that matters to a broad audience. Defining and measuring success needs to take technical and human factors into account.

1. **Reflect on your end game**
   - Imagine that your problem has gone away, or you have achieved your goal. How are you going to feel?
   - List the people who matter most in this context.
   - What do you want those people to say, see, think, feel or experience? Make a note of the answers.

2. **Ask 'What's the *most* important?'**
   - What are the most important things to accomplish in your organisation for this project work? What is the minimum you can deliver that will still leave you happy about the outcome?
   - Identify the importance of achievement for your people, the business outcomes and the amount and quality of work delivered.
   - Ask these questions to provoke discussion:
   - What are our customers' expectations?
   - What are the financial measures to get a return on investment?
   - Is it the end of the world if it delivers late?
   - Can we afford a budget overrun?
   - What is the right balance against your organisation's scorecard and what else might you need to consider?

3. **Ask 'What's good enough?'**
   - What is the tension or trade-off between the different success criteria? Prioritise them.
   - Rank your success criteria and add some commentary. For example, if the most important thing is to meet the timelines, then team satisfaction is going to have to give, because you've got to meet those deadlines.

4. **Publish your success criteria**
   - Ensure your project manager includes the success measures in regular project reporting.

At the start, cynical stakeholders, customers and team members may not believe a project is going to achieve what it sets out to do. This is an opportunity to set the project up for success by ensuring it focuses on desired outcomes. Park your ego at the door, invite those critics in and listen to their points of view. You can include this as part of your planning workshop. Try and listen without blame or judgement. Consider if any of the doom and gloom they talk about is really going to happen.

Taking the time to define success with your team makes it more meaningful and assists with decision-making.

ACTION STEPS › EXECUTING YOUR GAME PLAN AND MEASURING SUCCESS

You can work on this with a facilitator or your project manager. As the sponsor, you must chair the meeting.

1. **Use your roadmap**

    Every quarter, book a full day to review your previous 90 days, plan your next 90 days, and support your sub-teams to do the same. When planning, don't over-schedule things into one quarter. Remember the optimism bias.

2. **Review your routine activities**

    Some questions to ask:
    - Did you hold your planned meetings?
    - Are the learning activities well-attended?
    - Did you host an appreciation activity?

    What are your retrospective insights and lessons learned on how things can improve for the next cycle?

3. **Managing surprises**

    Did you have any surprises this quarter? How were they handled? Ask your team:
    - What went wrong?
    - Did we anticipate this problem?
    - What did we do to fix it?
    - Did we need additional funds to fix it?
    - Did we need to change our schedule?
    - Did the problem impact our project in a way that we had to replan the whole project?

4. **Measure your success**

    Check your progress against your agreed success criteria after each major stepping stone. Are you on track to achieve your outcomes? What else might you need to ensure success?

Progress check

When you put your game plan into action, you will be at Level Four on the sponsor productivity ladder.

Level	Sponsor behaviour	Project impact	
Five	Transforming	Kicking goals	
Four	Learning	Developing a game plan	Tipping point: Feedback
Three	Stable	Drills (routine)	
Two	Coping	Make a move	Tipping point: Decision
One	Paralysed	Out of the game	

Conclusion

Some sponsors and teams have an idea or an aspiration, but there is no realistic plan connected to it. You have to understand the steps that you and your team need to take to turn your ideas into reasonable plans, and turn those plans into reality.

Ensure your game plan is in place and the right work is prioritised. Connecting your purpose to the game plan helps you and your team keep going. Taking the time to plan a piece of work and define success with your team makes it more realistic and achievable. Planning does not need to be highly engineered to be useful. It is an essential ingredient in consistently achieving goals. It also teaches you how to set up an operating rhythm that suits your team.

Next steps

The next chapter discusses the importance of communication, including reaching out to your stakeholders. You've now got concrete plans in progress and you need to communicate that progress. People want to know what they're getting for their time, talent and money.

PART C

REFLECT

This final section is about courage and vulnerability. Now is the time to soar like an Eagle and look more broadly. Open yourself up to the critics. Put yourself out there. Build momentum and get to a flow state. You have been looking inwards at your team to get things to a stable state. Now it is time to look up and outwards to the broader landscape.

CHAPTER 11

Communicating with stakeholders

During your project, you need to keep your stakeholders informed about your progress and make it easy for them to find out the latest project news. This is also about controlling your project's story, ensuring information is not being manipulated or misused. In this chapter, we use visual management methods as the primary way to communicate progress. It's similar to a scoreboard at a sporting event. It is time-saving for the team and engaging for everyone.

Visual management methods convey complex information in an easy-to-read way. This summary makes life easier for executives who already have too much to digest. If your communications are too complicated, you risk them not being read and then not achieving the project outcomes. You don't want to waste people's time.

Progress reports also need to be read by stakeholders, in case there is something that impacts their business or other projects. For example, imagine you are sponsoring a home loan project and one of your key stakeholders is a mortgage broker. He has promised a new loan type for a particular date and has been telling his customers that this new loan is coming and it will change their lives. However, you are blocked on a key work item and the project is running two months behind schedule. That information is buried in a 50-page report, which he hasn't had time to read. If it had been on a visual management board, he would have been able to quickly see that the loan project was blocked – i.e. it had a major problem preventing the team's progress – and was running late.

If stakeholders get a nasty surprise, they can cause a firestorm and waste a great deal of your time. You and your team will be diverted to calming people down instead of focusing on delivering.

Most reports have an executive summary. These can be valuable, but many people do not read past the abstract. In the 2004 *Harvard Business Review* article, 'Stop Wasting Valuable Time', Michael Mankins has some great suggestions for executive reporting from Cadbury Schweppes.

> *'… all reading materials have been distributed to participants at least five days before each [Chief Executive Committee] session. Whenever possible, standard templates are used to display important financial, market, and competitor information. This gives each CEC member time to carefully review materials before the meeting and quickly get up to speed on important issues. Second, a standard cover sheet is included with all materials specifying precisely why people are being asked to read them – for information purposes only, for discussion and debate (in which case, the key issues are highlighted), or for making a decision and deciding a course of action.'*

The Australian Institute of Company Directors also talks about effective decision-making, and making sure that the information is succinct to make it easy to make decisions.

Visual management boards

A visual management board (VMB) is a physical space that is used to display your high-level purpose and plans. People will rally around the boards regularly as part of an inclusive routine to give and receive progress updates. As a sponsor, you and your team will be inviting stakeholders to provide constructive feedback on what's working and what's not working about the VMB.

This is Goldilocks communication: pragmatism over perfectionism. You don't spend hours preparing a report. Instead, you invite comments, questions and considerations when your stakeholders are present.

Any blank space you can write on and stick things to can be a canvas for your VMB. The physical space needs to be at least 1 m x 1 m. Any smaller and it's not particularly useful. I've seen some that are 3 m x 2 m. They are helpful for large programs. A reasonable size is a standard magnetic whiteboard that is about an arm's span in length.

There are two principal levels of project VMBs: the project level and the portfolio level. The project VMB is used for planning and running team drills. The portfolio level reflects a summary of the essential items on the project VMB.

Playground project

Purpose: A safe, accessible play space for 2–6-year-olds in central Newtown

To do (backlog)	In progress	Blocked	Completed (done)
Climbing frame assembly	Sandpit excavation – Bob	Slide assembly – Mo	Council Approvals
Swings assembly	See-saw assembly – Mo		Customer feedback
Flooring installation	Park bench assembly – Jack		Playground design
			Equipment ordered

SIMPLE PROJECT VMB

Newtown City Council projects portfolio

Purpose: A thriving community from birth to retirement

Project name	To do (backlog)	In progress	Blocked	Completed (done)
				Housing development stage 1 Project
Playground project Sponsor Project Manager			Equipment assembly	Regulatory approvals Community feedback Design Equipment ordered
Hospital development project Sponsor Project Manager	Plans Approvals			
Primary School development project	Fit-out Painting Landscaping Finishing	Building construction		Plans Approvals

Portfolio VMB example

A VMB shows your agreed work on the left side. The various work stages are spread across the board. It shows you what's blocked and what tasks people are doing. This allows the viewer to get vital information quickly. It's engaging because they're not just looking at a piece of paper or a screen. A VMB reinforces purpose and importance while increasing productivity, as progress is updated regularly and visibly. Your team members get valuable feedback.

A VMB is efficient – you can answer questions and sort out risks and issues quickly. You can have 15–30-minute standing status meetings. You stand, because it makes people get on with it and then move on. Every board is customisable by the team but should always clearly reflect current status and any issues (blockers) requiring decision-making. The recommended headers for the board types are shown above. You can read a lot more about how to design boards to suit you in the Agile Scrum and Kanban spaces. For information on Scrum or Kanban, check out scrumology.com and kanbanize.com.

This approach allows people to see how your weekly team drills are feeding into your overall plan. It brings those micro plans together to form a macro plan.

AN EARLY ADOPTER

Nigel Dalton, former CIO of Lonely Planet travel guides, was an inspiring advocate for the VMB. He got the technology team using data VMBs first. Eventually, the whole business was using them, including the accounting team and the marketing team. The boards were all customised. They came in all shapes and sizes and continued to be used for years after he left.

When you design your board, start by thinking who will be using it. The primary audience is the project team, who will use it to manage their tasks and activities. The secondary audience is the stakeholders. The VMB needs to benefit the team first and then the stakeholders, not the other way around. However, it also needs to be explained easily. With a little training, your stakeholders will be comfortable with how the information is presented.

The Toyota factory made Kanban boards famous in the 1940s. The idea was that you could look at any Kanban board in any Toyota factory and understand it. If you've worked in a team or attended a standing meeting, you can easily understand what work is progressing, and what's stopping them.

Remember that confidential and sensitive information needs special handling, for example, using secure rooms.

Setting up your VMB

As a sponsor, the VMBs are not yours to look after. It's your job to create the space and approve the wall or space for the team to set up the board, and it would help if you make it clear what information is essential to you. However, you want somebody else in the team – usually either the project manager or coach – to design and manage the board.

Invest in the whiteboard or wall space, approve the budget, support them to get it done and clear any internal logistical roadblocks. Be there when the team designs the board. Guide them to set it up within the four columns: backlog or to-do, in progress, blocked and done. Be very clear about what your definition of 'Done' is.

Ensure it is not over-engineered. You are trying to keep the communication simple enough for people to follow. If you've got a team member that likes more detail, give them the option to either develop a personal board or use a digital tool.

Ask your project manager or coach to organise standing meetings at set days and times each week. Make sure that the team has agreed to these. In the early stages, if they schedule daily standing meetings, you might need to go. Later you can attend at least one per week. Make sure they know when you will be there, so that if they need decisions to unblock issues urgently, they know they can raise that with you in the meeting. Ask questions like, 'How are you doing? Do you need any help? What does that mean?' Invite them to ask you questions too.

Your expected weekly time commitment is 15 minutes, 2–3 times a week, or 30 minutes, 1–2 times a week.

If you have a virtual team spread across different time zones, this can be challenging. One way to address this is to use a digital collaboration tool. One example is Trello, which looks identical to a VMB. You can also replicate physical VMBs in the different locations. Set up video links when you hold your standing meetings, and show that you've got identical boards.

Digital tools are handy for managing large complex programs, and they make it easy to track and update the information. But if you're going to go down the digital path for tracking and reporting, you will need someone whose primary job is to manage that information. Otherwise, the data will get out of control and be useless.

Inclusive routines and rituals

At the core of this method are regular progress meetings (stand-ups), the reflection sessions (retrospectives) and demonstration sessions or showcases (discussed later in this chapter). These are simple ways to inform your stakeholders about your project.

During the retrospectives, you ask your team what's working and what needs improving. Similarly, when your stakeholders look at what you're doing, ask them what they think of the VMB. What did they find valuable? What's working for them? What needs improving? Choose the feedback that you find useful.

While the VMB is partly about controlling the project, its primary purpose is about communicating. You're giving your stakeholders an understanding of what's going on with your team. Your routines and rituals need to be inclusive. Invite your stakeholders, particularly if they've got questions or they're seen as troublemakers. Ask them to attend and show them what you're doing. It promotes transparency.

Regular scheduling of these meetings means that people can more easily commit and attend as they need to. The routine and ritual are vital parts of keeping communication open and engaging people.

ROUTINE MEETINGS YIELD RESULTS

One operations team had a daily 8.30 am huddle. The group gathered around their Kanban board to balance their workload and address critical customer issues. Anyone from the organisation was invited to join, listen, ask questions and offer suggestions or solutions. This was particularly useful when they had a significant incident – for example, if something had gone wrong with the software system and was impacting lots of clients. The CEO often joined them and helped with problem-solving.

Another project team at a large bank was looking at technology risk. At one point, all the ATMs had a standard set of keys. The keys were made available illegally on eBay and people were opening ATMs and taking customer cards that had been retained by the machine. The team solved that problem during their meetings.

Showcases

The purpose of a showcase is for project teams to demonstrate prototypes to their stakeholders and get their feedback. In a showcase, you're physically demonstrating what you've created so far. It might be software, a product prototype, a process or procedure. These sessions also promote transparency while addressing stakeholder concerns and increasing engagement.

Showcases are slightly longer than retrospectives, typically 30–45 minutes.

Sometimes teams use posters, slide decks or 'imagine if' stories to describe a prototype or product. Don't hold a showcase if you have nothing concrete to show. What is the point? You've promised to demonstrate a working prototype – if you don't display something real, you'll make the situation worse. You risk losing credibility and engagement.

A well-run showcase where you're showing something tangible is the easiest way to reduce noise from your critics. Ask the team to publish the timetable for your showcases on your intranet or put up posters in the lunchroom. Spread the information by word of mouth, invite your stakeholders and encourage them to ask questions. People who have been wondering what you have been up to will realise you are producing something. And unhelpful critics tend to go quiet in the face of progress.

Ask your project manager to schedule showcases every 4–6 weeks. Don't go longer, because people may think that your project's in trouble. **Caution: On top-secret projects, be careful who you invite to your showcases.**

Establishing communication forums

Identify your communication channels

Ask your project manager to check what critical project communication channels are available in your organisation. These could include social media channels, posters and email invitations. For example, some organisations use a Microsoft tool called Yammer to put out information. Some people like signs in the tearoom. Word-of-mouth invitations from project champions (stakeholders who are passionate about the project) are popular. Figure out what will work in your organisation.

Publish a communication calendar for your stakeholders
Ask your project manager to ensure there is a published calendar for your standing meetings, retrospectives and showcases, using whichever communication channels you prefer.

Invite your stakeholders to your communication events
Make a habit of inviting people to your progress meetings and showcases every month. Some people like the personal touch.

Encourage attendance
It may be hard to get some stakeholders to attend. At the start of your project, you and your project manager will have identified the key stakeholders. They've got skin in the game, and they will care about the project outcome. Make it easy for them to turn up. Consult them about suitable times and get the invitations sent from the most senior stakeholder. In most cases, that will be the sponsor. Ask someone in your team to send reminders and keep a register of attendance.

> **THE CEO ENCOURAGES ATTENDANCE**
>
> In one organisation, the CEO showed support by attending communication forums. He made time and turned up to forums regularly and encouraged his leadership team to attend. Within a month, several of his executive leaders started coming to relevant forums. This increased their understanding of what the projects were striving to achieve for their business, improved team morale and more work was done at a faster pace.

Consider how to manage people who consistently don't attend. Are you going to escalate, influence or ignore? Your response will depend on how influential that person is. If they're not a significant influencer or decision-maker, and they can't derail your project, make them an optional attendee. Focus on the people who are most important and get them in the door.

Ask for feedback

After the showcase or meeting, ask for feedback to find out what your stakeholders found useful, even if you only ask one person each time. It will only take a minute.

Inviting and acting on stakeholder feedback

You don't have to accept and act on every bit of feedback. However, you do need to know if you're hitting the mark with your stakeholders. Make sure that they understand the VMB, the showcases and the key messages you're trying to communicate.

You can evolve your board based on that feedback, but keep it simple. If you make it too complicated, you will lose people's attention.

FEEDBACK IMPROVES A VMB

One projects portfolio had a VMB that had been running for about eight weeks. They were getting regular drop-ins. The CEO and other senior stakeholders would turn up, listen patiently and, at the end of the meeting, ask questions like, 'What does this heading mean?' If it wasn't easily explainable, the heading was adjusted.

The VMB evolved, with three significant redesigns over time. One project was a risk program that ended up being the number one project. The risk program lead noticed that there wasn't enough information on the VMB to satisfy her stakeholders. She got her stakeholders involved in designing a new VMB that worked for that program. This approach worked exceptionally well.

Imagine an initiative where the team needs to develop new product packaging and instructions. Progress halts because a team member is waiting for someone in the design department to come back to them. The initiative is in the 'Blocked' column, and your team physically can't progress any design work. At the meeting, your stakeholders see that the packaging is blocked, and you inform them about the reasons for the hold-up. The stakeholders might be able to help. Later, they might say, 'I found that meeting useful because I was able to help somebody. And now I understand how many things can hold your process up.'

A stakeholder might say that they didn't find it useful to hear about technology defects. 'Can we have a special meeting for that – I don't want to hear about it and I don't understand it. Do I need to be there?' Your response might be, 'I'm sorry, but that's an important part of this initiative. Over time, you will understand it.' You could also find a way of negotiating if you really need them at those meetings.

People may not offer feedback for fear of recrimination or loss of relationships. This is especially likely if they don't understand or don't like something. As a sponsor, the best thing you can do is listen to the feedback, in whatever way it is phrased, and offer them confidentiality.

For example, a stakeholder may not want to provide feedback in an open forum. They might be worried about upsetting a software developer who is key to the project. Invite them to have a confidential chat and say what they think. This gives you an opportunity as an Owl sponsor to coach the developer. You must provide protection and follow through with the offer of confidentiality. Don't invite it and then crucify the person that is giving you feedback.

Another approach is to invite people to give anonymous feedback. This is a weaker option – when people provide anonymous reviews, they can often lack empathy. It also doesn't allow you to ask additional questions to understand the meaning of the feedback. However, if you can assume positive intent, any feedback is better than none. The quality will improve over time.

Types of feedback

There are four types of stakeholder feedback. The first is from your fans. They won't criticise you at all. They'll love you and your work, and they'll turn up to whatever you do.

Then there's the feedback from trolls and jellyfish. Nothing you do will satisfy them. Trolls want to throw rocks, no matter what. Jellyfish will make mean comments while pretending to be friendly. You need to put a fence around those unhelpful critics and leave them behind. They're trying to make you do a whole lot of work that's not adding value to your overall project. You could spend hours and days satisfying one wish. Work out what is going to be valuable and contributes to achieving your project's vision.

The most useful feedback comes from the helpful critics. They might not like something, but they still want you to succeed. They asking decent questions like, 'Help me to understand that,' or, 'This isn't working for me. I'd like to see this.'

	Unhelpful	Helpful
Friendly	Jellyfish	Fans
Unfriendly	Trolls	Critics

If you're thick-skinned enough, take all the feedback on board and filter it. If you don't like the way that the feedback has been expressed, ask them to repeat it more respectfully and constructively. Say in a calm and gentle tone, 'You may not have realised it, but I found that comment disrespectful. Could you please rephrase that?' Sometimes the feedback is useful, but has been poorly communicated.

This happens a lot with technology people. They get immersed in jargon. I've heard a stakeholder say to a technologist, 'You talk too much and lose me in your technical explanations.' Let them know when you don't like how they're saying it. However, continue to invite constructive feedback. You want to keep people engaged and feeling safe.

ACTION STEPS ▸ CONDUCTING REGULAR STAKEHOLDER MEETINGS

1. **Create ground rules**
   Ask your project manager to work with the team to establish your meeting ground rules. When, where and how often are you going to meet? How long will each person's update be? The most effective stand-ups cap each person's contribution to two minutes. What are your standard questions? The questions that often work best are, 'Do you need any help?' and 'Are you blocked on anything?'

2. **Show up consistently**
   Meet at the board at the agreed time. Start the meeting on time, every time. Punctuality demonstrates that you mean business and intend to be consistent. As the sponsor, if you are punctual, you set the tone. Everyone else will conform after two or three meetings.

3. **One conversation at a time**
   Use a token as a talking stick. The person with the talking stick is the one giving their update. One team uses a fluffy toy cheetah as a token.

4. **Listen first, talk last**
   Listen to each team member giving their updates. Your role as the sponsor is to listen to the team and offer help. Once you've heard the updates, provide yours. By going last, you may discover answers to the issues you wanted to raise, and you can adjust your update as a result. Ask the team 'What help do you need from me?'

5. **Improve the next meeting**
   Ask your observers and critics, 'What did you find most useful? What could be improved?' If there are lots of suggestions, narrow it down to what the three most important. Remember to thank people for taking the time to provide feedback.

Conclusion

You can use these communication tools and methods to create a safe, accessible environment for your stakeholders and find out what's really going on in your projects. They build trust and lasting collaboration. You understand how to use a visual tool to communicate the key messages of a project and portfolio and how to use a showcase to demonstrate progress, show real results, effectively involve your stakeholders and get useful feedback without feeling overwhelmed.

Next steps

In the next chapter, we look at how to recover from setbacks on your sponsor journey so that you can keep going with confidence and show progress to your stakeholders.

CHAPTER 12

Keep the faith

Projects take time, money and energy. With long and complex projects, it's common to get disheartened. With transformation projects, you don't have a choice to go back to where you started. You've got to go forward – the bridges behind you have been burnt. So, how do you keep the faith?

When you're clear on where you're going and why, it's much harder to get thrown off course. This is the guiding light from the roadmap you created in Chapter 9. The challenge is that you don't know what surprises are in store.

In this chapter, you will learn some useful techniques to recover from setbacks. At the end, you will map your progress against the roadmap so you can keep your team, and yourself, focused on achieving your shared outcome.

Recovering from setbacks

No project will always run smoothly, no matter how well-planned it is. What do you do when you encounter setbacks? What do the obstacles look like? It's important to acknowledge that a problem has arisen. Don't just dismiss it. Move forward with a plan and take positive action.

WEBSITE LAUNCHES WITH SLOW PERFORMANCE

A major IT project for a financial services organisation developed a new website and technology platform to look after investments, superannuation and insurances. On the new website, one performance measure was that the system responded in under 11 seconds to a client clicking on a link. (We wouldn't put up with that today, but it was acceptable back then.)

When the website was launched, many of the functions took more than 60 seconds to respond, or timed out. It was a complete disaster. Within 48 hours, the website had to be shut down. Clients and advisers were diverted to the old site. The organisation hadn't expected to keep the old site running, but they had no choice. A separate project was run specifically to address the performance issues. No one was happy about it. It took a lot of money and six months to resolve. The relaunch went well and, after a few months, people got over the horrible experience.

The critical point is that it did take a while to recover. A lot of people felt angry and upset, and wanted to distance themselves from the project. A calm and gutsy Eagle sponsor was assigned. She hired a fearless project manager to sort out those performance issues. She provided him with appropriate protection and direction. He was calm and steadfast. If he had lost his cool, all faith would have been lost and the team's effort would have been wasted.

You can rebuild if you keep going, improve and recover from the setback.

It's important to express empathy, and to give yourself a break as the sponsor too. You can say, 'I'm sorry that this has happened,' or 'This sucks'. Don't wallow for too long, though. Focus on solving the problem.

In a TED Talk called 'The surprising science of happiness', Dan Gilbert says, 'You find a way to be happy with what's happened.' He gives examples of the science behind synthetic happiness, including case studies on a person winning the lottery and a person becoming a paraplegic. In the immediate aftermath, the lottery winner is ecstatic and the paraplegic is unhappy. But, surprisingly, 12 months after the respective events, both the paraplegic and the lottery winner are equally content. The critical point is that we tend to find a way to accept and adjust to any situation, so that we can be happy and get on with our lives.

Project managers with more than two years' experience are used to things not going to plan. They say, 'That sucked. What do we do? Just get on with it.' Any executive leader or sponsor who wants to bounce back must have grit, resilience and determination. 'That was really awful. But I had all these people who helped me.'

You learn a lot more from failure than from success.

THE WATERMELON PROJECT

> Robin was sponsoring a project and her project manager was telling her that everything was fine. They were getting close to the technology implementation date. But this was what is sometimes called a watermelon project – green on the outside, but red on the inside. It all looked fine, but it was

not good. The project manager was inexperienced and was hiding issues and information and pretending everything was okay. None of the work met quality expectations. It was going to take months and a lot of money to fix it. Robin was unpleasantly surprised. Had she been an Ostrich on this project?

Robin acknowledged her emotions, which included anger, frustration and disappointment. She recognised that, as a sponsor, she was responsible, even though her project manager had been ineffective. She took ownership of this and did not blame others. Accepting responsibility and getting to the root cause does take guts. Robin said, 'I wasn't asking the right questions. I needed to dig deeper and ask for more proof points.'

She reached out to the technology head and her project coach for help and advice. She planned the way out of the mess with her team and advisers. They used a process similar to the payoff matrix – brainstorming and writing down options on cards. Robin put options up on the wall, stepped back, looked at which options were acceptable, and which could be achieved within the available time. She made a decision on the most useful thing to do at that point in time.

Robin was a brave Eagle sponsor. She acted and didn't overthink it. She updated her plan and schedule with the team, and they recovered the project and delivered it.

The process described in the case study above assumes that you're not out of time and that you can call on extra money or skilled people to address the setbacks. You might need to work through some of these options. When you did your planning in Chapter 9, you would have set aside money and time for surprises. In many project methodologies, that is called contingency funding.

In the unlikely event that there have been a lot of surprises, you may have reached an impasse. In that situation, this four-step strategy will help.

Prioritise

Look at other projects being run by other sponsors. You might need to go up the food chain, prioritise your project over others in your organisation and take their funding. To achieve this, you will need to have either a transparent prioritisation process (like the one outlined in Chapter 4), healthy relationships with your other sponsors or strong advocacy from your executive sponsor.

Adjust

If it's within your control, you could advise up the chain that you need to change your plans to accommodate the additional work or the setback. You might need to reduce the project's scope or remove some items and deliver less than you initially planned.

Wait

You might need to put your project on hold until you have funding and people available. This is often the worst option, as you lose momentum. People will work on other things while you're waiting, and it takes time to get back up to speed when you do return. Also, if the setback has happened very close to when you're planning to go live, waiting may not be an option.

Kill

The bravest option, if it's the lowest value project in the overall portfolio, is to write the project off. This take guts but can often be better than limping along.

In a mature organisation where people are used to doing projects, the last two will rarely happen. If you're new to projects and you're building up your project sponsor capability and project management knowledge, these can occur but are much more likely to happen in the early stages of a project's life.

Sometimes a problem is beyond the skill of the project team to fix. Things like changes in legislation can derail projects. That doesn't mean you lose faith. Your job, as a courageous sponsor, is to say, 'Even if we follow all the prescriptive steps in this way of working, sometimes things are beyond us.' This is the reality of projects. The goal is to make sure that if Wait or Kill are options, they come at the very beginning of your project.

Update progress against your roadmap

Make sure that you map your progress against the roadmap you created in Chapter 9. This allows you and your team to step back and see the bigger picture. It can be difficult to see progress when you're in the thick of it. Updating your progress against your roadmap will keep everyone encouraged and uplifted and help them keep going.

It's tough for anyone to argue against data and statistics. If you don't keep track of your progress, it becomes harder to prove that your project is a worthwhile investment.

It's very similar to a weight-loss program. If you don't weigh yourself at the start, it's easy to say you've lost weight just by judging your emotions. It's more useful to record your starting weight and measurements, then track your progress.

Setting a goal and having a clear set of measures gives you focus.

You know where you're going and you know when you've achieved each step, because you can tick it off against your success criteria.

Keep it simple. Prioritise what's important and helpful to you. If having a lot of data is important, keep it but don't update it against your roadmap. Invest in a digital tool to record the extra details. If you put all the detail on your chart, it becomes impossible to see what you are recording your progress against – there's too much information. Keep your roadmap clear and easy to read.

ROADMAP UPDATED WITH COMPLETED PROJECT WORK AND SURPRISES

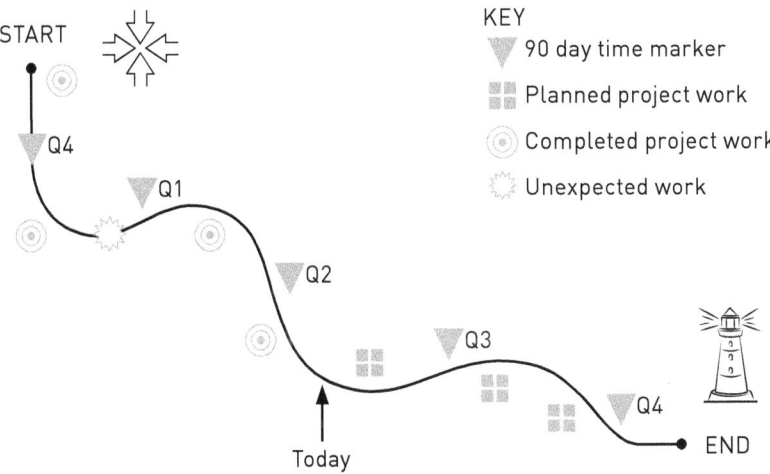

Resist changing your baseline – it meddles with the integrity of the data. That is short-term thinking and will not help you in the long run. When people fiddle with the baseline, they are trying to say that they're achieving when they're not: something's coming in within budget, being delivered at the scheduled time, or providing all the scope items they agreed to. They do it to make themselves feel better.

It is much better to accept when you haven't quite hit the mark or have fallen short.

While there are legitimate reasons to rebaseline, they must not be decided arbitrarily. They need to be discussed with experienced people outside your project; for example, your project management office.

IMPACTS OF FALSE REPORTING

One technology program had a budget of $1,200,000 and an estimated completion time of nine months. The developers hit technical difficulties and had to work overtime but their manager asked them to record a maximum of eight hours a day on their weekly timesheets. Some of the developers worked an additional seven hours a day.

The project finished on time and under budget, and the manager made his bonus. The data was then used as a guideline for the next project's time and cost estimates. Given that these were wrong by a factor of at least 50%, that set the next sponsor and project team up for failure. The first team had meddled with the baseline.

It's human nature to want to adjust things in your favour. People alter the baselines of success measures all the time. This is usually for one of two reasons. The first is that the baseline is tied to a performance scorecard and the team want to get your bonus or reward. The second is about not losing face.

Perhaps the best response is to reward honesty and integrity over exact numerical goals.

ACTION STEPS ▶ SHOW PROGRESS AGAINST YOUR ROADMAP

1. **Update your roadmap to show progress**
   Use the roadmap that you created in Chapter 9. Update it monthly and get the work done. Describe your progress in your newsletters or information session, as detailed in Chapter 11.

2. **Show the surprises**
   From a sponsor perspective, explain how issues came about and how your team tackled them and got back on track. If further details are required, invite your project manager and team to contribute.

3. **Celebrate**
   Celebrate your recovery from setbacks. Cheering and saying 'Well done' and 'Thank you' are often enough.

Progress check

You have now reached Level Five on the sponsor productivity ladder.

Level	Sponsor behaviour	Project impact	
Five	Transforming	Kicking goals	
Four	Learning	Developing a game plan	Tipping point: Feedback
Three	Stable	Drills (routine)	
Two	Coping	Make a move	Tipping point: Decision
One	Paralysed	Out of the game	

Conclusion

In this chapter, we've discussed strategies for bouncing back after a setback and the importance of updating your progress in a simple way against your roadmap.

You need ongoing advocacy and support from your bosses and your team. This is a transformation movement. You, as a sponsor, and your stakeholders need to be able to actively engage your fans and critics and have a response for your unkind critics.

Be kind to yourself and your team when you hit an obstacle. Focus on moving forward and using your roadmap. See the bigger picture and involve your stakeholders in your overall transformation journey.

Next steps

In the next chapter, we will talk about taking your game to the next level. You're now in a steady operating rhythm and are kicking goals. What level do you want to go to next?

CHAPTER 13

Taking your game to the next level

Throughout this book, you have learnt processes and how to establish good habits. Now you can take those experiences and add a dash more courage to take your game to the next level and become a consistent Owl sponsor.

This means using continuous improvement practices and taking strategic risks to take advantage of growth opportunities. Incremental innovation helps you stay relevant to your customers, stay in business and advance your career. Continuous improvement provides stability for your employees and confidence for your stakeholders.

This quote is attributed to Winston Churchill: 'Success is not final, failure is not fatal. It is the courage to continue that counts.' If you're not brave and don't put in place strategies to take you to the next level, you risk slipping back down the sponsor productivity ladder. If you want to keep transforming, you can't use the same game plan forever.

STEVE JOBS ▸ PERSISTENT INNOVATOR

> Steve Jobs started Apple in his garage. He built an empire, then had an almighty fall from grace when he was sacked as CEO by his board. But Apple didn't do quite so well without him. He learned some lessons and was eventually brought back in, inventing the iPod and iPad on his return. He rose, fell and was resurrected. He continued to do incremental innovation and took the company to even greater success.

Stanford University's Centre for Assessment, Learning and Equity seeks to improve instruction and learning through the design and development of innovative, educative, state-of-the-art performance assessments. Stanford has this approach to scaling: 'Scaling requires not only fidelity to core processes and programs but also constant adjustments to local needs and resources.' Your foundations may be solid, but change is constant so you will need to evolve as new things arise.

In this chapter, we will look at a continuous improvement mindset including practices, processes and pragmatic courage. Together, these form your growth framework.

We also look at stories from sponsorship forums – both cautionary and celebratory. When you place stories at the centre of your project's narrative, they become ingrained in your organisation's memory. They help us remember and understand our past and make us better equipped for decision-making and courageous leaps of faith.

Continuous improvement mindset

The continuous improvement mindset helps you maintain standards and good habits. Without regularly scheduled maintenance, when your program gets bigger, bad habits tend to erode your benchmarks. This erosion undermines the quality of the work you deliver and your associated reporting. When you don't have time scheduled for maintenance, it's easy to get lost in activities and forget about it.

Scheduling project maintenance once a quarter will contribute positively to your efficiency, quality, productivity and the wellbeing of both you and your team. Regular maintenance then becomes your usual way of working and provides stability while looking after the people side of things.

Toyota have specialised trainers and each factory has a dojo –a martial arts term for a training space. The trainers are trained in Japan, then they train the staff on the factory floor in their respective dojos. Trainers are sent back to headquarters every three months to undo any bad habits and learn new standards. We are all human and we do pick up bad habits and take shortcuts. Sometimes we need to review and challenge these habits, keeping the good ones and discarding the bad.

If there are lots of things that need attention, you may have no idea where to start. Address this by prioritising your non-negotiable maintenance items, defining what standard you want to maintain them, and focusing on those. Make sure you have an investment business case and that you run your daily stand-ups and monthly governance oversight forums. Make sure that you're maintaining those and that they're working well. If you've got the capacity and the will to do more, add those progressively.

Continuous improvement practices

Standards

Support your team with time and a small budget to define standards for their work and either join or set up learning communities of practice. Define these standards after you've had some experience, and you've learned from your successes and failures.

Define 'done'

You and your team need to agree on the definition of 'done'. 'Done' is usually when the work is completed to an acceptable quality. Without universal definitions, we make up our own.

Community of practice

Join or set up a learning community of practice. You will typically find at least one person in your team that is delighted to do this. Appoint them to organise the community and the events. It can be as simple as having a guest once a month to talk on a relevant topic that's useful for you and your transformation project. Let your team decide what other topics are needed. It's all about enhancing your team drills and improving quality while you're working.

Innovation and risk-taking

You need to understand your appetite for risk. On one hand, you don't want to take foolhardy risks and go across a tightrope without a net. On the other hand, if you're not trying something new, you will stay where you are.

Every sponsor is required to be a brave decision-maker on strategic projects – mainly to remain relevant to customers and increase benefit to the organisation and your people. Standard terms are profitability, efficiency and staff engagement. Courage will enable you to go to the next level.

RICHARD BRANSON ▶ INNOVATIVE RISK-TAKER

Richard Branson is a famous sponsor. He started his career in his mother's garage, selling records through newspaper ads. Now he does everything. He has both a personal brand and the Virgin brand. He's been courageous and pioneering on several different fronts. With Virgin, he went from selling records from his mum's garage to establishing one of the largest music stores, and then diversifying.

It didn't happen overnight. As Branson nudged his way to the megastore, he attracted investors and took risks. Not all his ventures have been successful. He's had many challenges, such as his airline venture and Virgin Galactic. He was persistent and consistent, and manages his personal brand well.

Branson is a fearless individual and a great example of a courageous sponsor.

You need to take innovation risks – if there's no risk, there's no reward. In investment terms, cash is the safest instrument. You can stick it under your mattress or put it into a low-interest investment, but you're probably going to lose money over time. Low risk and low reward. Or you can move up to riskier investments, like property and equities, with greater risk but greater potential reward.

Use a decision register and try to avoid knee-jerk reactions. Think it through, make sure that it's within your risk appetite, and then make a move. A snap judgement made under pressure is often the wrong thing to do.

Your organisation will probably have a set risk appetite that uses a framework. This will have been set with your executive team in the context of the broader organisation and your industry regulators. This will keep you safe from risk-taking under pressure. The Australian Government Department of Finance has an excellent information sheet that explains how to define risk appetite and tolerance.

A risk appetite statement for a bank would contain elements like liquidity positions, how much capital will be invested in projects, balanced scorecards and ethical obligations. It's not all about finance. A lot of organisations talk about the triple bottom line, where they support practices that are good for the environment as well as the shareholders and the customers.

This framework tells you what you can take a risk on. For example, some organisations might decide that their technology hardware will last for five or six years, while others would replace it after four years. They're prepared to take that risk.

When you're facing a new opportunity, you need to perform a courage assessment. Is this initiative an opportunity to exploit or a threat to mitigate? Ask, 'What is the likelihood that we will be able to realise this? What value is this going to return? How easy is it for us to do this?'

When you've worked that out, ask, 'What is the benefit to our organisation, customers and staff if we do realise this? What is it going to give us in terms of revenue, reputation, etc?' Think about what is essential to your organisation. Focus on pursuing high-benefit, high-likelihood opportunities. Ensure that they are within your set risk appetite and are not too risky to pursue.

In terms of threats, is it easy to get very alarmed very quickly. Focus on spreading the risk. For example, many banks have a 'three-campus model', so they can continue operating if one building becomes unusable after a terror attack. What is the likelihood that the threat will eventuate? What damage might it cause if it does happen? While a terror attack might be highly unlikely, you wouldn't recover from the trauma if it did happen. Focus on addressing severe damage and high-likelihood threats. Ensure these are within your set risk appetite, and that you aren't chasing unrealistic stuff.

When you've identified your opportunities and threats, repeat the prioritisation process using the payoff matrix tool in Chapter 4, and choose the strategic opportunities you will pursue.

This will be challenging if your decision-makers and influencers are at different ends of the risk spectrum. The best way to diffuse this situation is to ask the risk-takers, 'Does this fall within our risk appetite?' Then ask the others, 'How can I develop my courage within this profile?'

To be truly courageous, you must take pragmatic risks.

Sharing knowledge

The PMI talks about communities of practice being an excellent way of advancing the way people work together. Sharing knowledge teaches things you can't get from reading a book.

Critics might say, 'Will people share their stories authentically'? Senior leaders often want to save face and look good in front of their peers. Address this by asking an experienced sponsor or facilitator to chair your forum. They will set the ground rules and guide the conversation. A brave chair who shares their war stories paves the way for the others to open up.

SPONSOR FORUMS ▸ SHARING STORIES FOR THE NEXT GENERATION OF SPONSORS

Sponsor forums are an opportunity for leaders to learn from their peers which successes to replicate and which pitfalls to avoid. It also encourages them to have fun. It builds confidence and courage and saves time, money and heartache on projects.

At one sponsor forum, a Duck sponsor expressed her frustration at the poor treatment she experienced at a governance funding forum. This is the forum where the sponsor presents the project business case to receive money for the project to proceed. 'I feel like I'm being attacked! I don't turn up at work to do a bad job. Can I just have some empathy and respect?' Some of the sponsor forum attendees were also on her governance funding forum. They were taken aback and agreed to modify their approach. In catching up with a community of her peers, she learned what happens when you exchange problems and ideas, and the governance forum became more empathetic and supportive towards new sponsors.

Another example is Scott Sears, who set up a community of practice at Boeing. Boeing has plants all over the world. They have communities of practice for project managers and sponsors where people get together and share their stories.

ACTION STEPS › CONTINUOUS IMPROVEMENT PRACTICES

1. **Schedule bi-monthly sponsor forums**

   Organise a 1–2-hour forum every two months. Hold it in a private room and make it invitation only, so you create a safe space to share. Establish the ground rules. Sharing a failure in the context of overall success will protect you from those who might use such a forum to undermine you.

   Sponsors showcasing their projects work very well. They're often very proud about talking about things that are going well. They're also pretty good about sharing experiences they've recovered from. It shows bravery to ask your peers for help. Get people's opinions, but also pass your tips on.

   If it's appropriate, record the information and share it with other sponsors. If it's not, anonymise it and share it (with permission). You are encouraging people to learn, not trying to shame them. Use humour to put failures in context. Highlight patterns or trends to share with the overall organisation, if you can and if it's allowed.

2. **Schedule quarterly innovation days**

   Executives always talk about time poverty. As a sponsor, you often get last-minute demands from executive management to solve a problem. Get your executive management on board, and ask them to prioritise their time. You'll soon see results.

Conclusion

We've looked at how to establish and maintain good habits for continuous improvement, how to test if a growth opportunity is worth the risk and the courage it will take, plus how to set up an environment for sponsors to share stories and continue to grow their capability.

To get to the continuous improvement stage, you need to be past the stable phase and your team drills need to be delivering value. Try this approach for three to six months. In the fifth month, if it's not working, get an independent review. There may be something else, such as culture challenges, going on. Get improvement recommendations from the project management expert who is helping you conduct the investigation.

Next steps

Decide what your minimum standards are and apply continuous improvement practices to those. Understand your risk appetite and find the courage to explore new growth opportunities. Establish sponsor forums, both formal and informal, for sponsors to share their experiences.

You are now be doing everything required of an Owl sponsor and can positively contribute to the world of project management, achieving outstanding outcomes.

CHAPTER 14

The road ahead

This book has given you insights and actions, as well as distinctions between old ways of doing things and new techniques. You used to be overwhelmed, but now you no longer have to be. You're confident, you're stable and you can get on and kick goals.

To get yourself unstuck and back to healthy productivity and progress, take a breath and meet with your team. My top tip is to be less of a hard-driving whip cracker and more of an inspiring leader and coach. Be present. Let your team get to know you as a person. Show them you care about them as well as about the outcome. Mentor them and help them understand your business. You'll get amazing results.

You can learn anything from anyone, so be brave and ask your team for help. Provide your team and stakeholders the necessary Eagle sponsor direction, protection and order. Focus on your end goal and bring people with you. Don't forget to record and measure your progress along the way. Proudly say, 'Look how far we've come'.

Make some time every day and every week to look for ways to learn and continuously improve. But don't forget your humanity. Have fun along the way.

Be brave and you will succeed. You cannot please everyone if you want to get progress and real results. The brave always find a way to be firm with their priorities and focus on finishing. Courage is the quickest, most straightforward way to tackle the complexities of project sponsorship. When you lead with courage, others follow with joy. Together, you will get a fantastic result.

You are now equipped to understand your team and able to clearly explain your goals. When you encounter obstacles, which you inevitably will, they will no longer have the power to unseat you. You can approach project problem-solving from a position of mutual respect. Your team will follow you by offering their commitment and effort, and will go above and beyond your expectations.

My wish for the world of projects is that sponsors develop the skills and behaviour they need to be successful and save themselves time, money and energy. I would be delighted if all sponsors became effective Eagle sponsors as a minimum, providing direction, protection and order to their teams.

I would love all sponsors to show a level of courage and care to their project teams. When your team is suffering, get down into the pit with them, take them by the hand and bring them back up the ladder to terra firma and sunshine.

COURAGEOUS SPONSOR TOP TIPS

- [ ] 90% of the job is showing up. It is proof that you care, that the project is valuable and that the team matters.

- [ ] Work on your project priorities and let unimportant things go.

- [ ] Model appropriate behaviour and set the tone for the team. Commend people for positive conduct. Be brave and have empathetic, solution-focused conversations with underperforming team members.

- [ ] Continuously build your network of trusted advisers. Ask for help when you need it.

- [ ] Prevent yourself from falling back into bad habits by taking a day every three months or so to take a critical look at how you might have lapsed.

- [ ] From each experience, no matter how rewarding or how horrible, ask, 'What have I learned and how can I improve next time?'

Further material

Books

Angela Duckworth, *Grit: The Power of Passion and Perseverance*, Ebury Publishing, 2017

Stephen Covey, *The Seven Habits of Highly Effective People*, Simon & Schuster, 2009

Carol Dweck, *Mindset: The New Psychology of Success*, Random House, 2008

Simon Sinek, *Start with Why: How Great Leaders Inspire Everyone to Take Action*, Penguin, 2011

Websites

Kanban › www.kanbanize.com

Project Management Institute › www.pmi.org

Scrumology › www.scrumology.com

Acknowledgements

This book began as a big idea to empower project sponsors to gain confidence and knowledge to champion their projects. I love it when sponsors 'get it' and start to get great results.

But how to turn this advice into a book? I am used to coaching and training, where I am always available to answer questions. Writing a book was a very different challenge. I had no idea where to start until I was introduced to my book coach, Kath Walters. She gave me structure, encouragement and advice and helped me turn these sponsor stories and research into a cohesive collection.

I enjoyed doing the research for the book. Along the way, many people have helped.

Firstly, thank you to my husband, Ed Sheehan, for giving me the space to write this book. Also for his perspective and insights as, at the time of writing, he was a full-time sponsor on a $100+ million technology program.

Thank you also to the following people for contributing content to this book:

Eduardo P Braun, author of *People First Leadership*, for excerpts from his interviews with Colin Powell; Antonio Nieto-Rodriguez, author of *The Project Revolution* and previous PMI Board Chair for excerpts from his hierarchy of purpose article. Antonio was also an early reviewer and gave me some fantastic encouragement.

Thank you to my other beta readers, who were encouraging and gave me a few steers and their own pearls of wisdom from the field:

Alex Danischewski AM, a former project director and Wing Commander, Australian Air Force (retired), and one of my early mentors; Tim Mitchell-Adams, financial services executive and experienced sponsor; and fellow experienced project professionals, David Rullmann, Susan McKenzie and Jenny Honig.

www.ingramcontent.com/pod-product-compliance
Ingram Content Group UK Ltd.
Pitfield, Milton Keynes, MK11 3LW, UK
UKHW021303180426
11947UKWH00015B/979